Working The Street

ALSO BY ERIK BANKS

The Financial Lexicon, Palgrave Macmillan, 2004.

Liquidity Risk. Palgrave Macmillan, 2004.

The Failure of Wall Street. Palgrave Macmillan, 2004.

The Credit Risk of Complex Derivatives, 3rd edition. Palgrave Macmillan, 2003.

Corporate Governance. Palgrave Macmillan, 2003.

Alternative Risk Transfer. John Wiley, 2004.

Exchange-Traded Derivatives. John Wiley, 2003.

The Simple Rules of Risk. John Wiley, 2002.

e-Finance. John Wiley, 2000.

The Rise and Fall of the Merchant Banks. Kogan Page, 1999.

The Credit Risk of Complex Derivatives, 2nd edition. Macmillan, 1997.

Asia Pacific Derivative Markets. Macmillan, 1996.

Emerging Asian Fixed Income Markets. Macmillan, 1995.

The Credit Risk of Complex Derivatives. Macmillan, 1994.

The Credit Risk of Financial Instruments. Macmillan, 1993.

AS CO-AUTHOR

Practical Risk Management (co-written with R. Dunn). John Wiley, 2003.

Weather Risk Management (edited/co-written with XL/Element Re).
     Palgrave Macmillan, 2001.

Working The Street

What You Need to Know About Life on Wall Street

Erik Banks

First published 2004 by
PALGRAVE MACMILLAN™
175 Fifth Avenue, New York, N.Y. 10010 and
Houndmills, Basingstoke, Hampshire, England RG21 6XS.
Companies and representatives throughout the world.

PALGRAVE MACMILLAN is the global academic imprint of the Palgrave Macmillan division of St. Martin's Press, LLC and of Palgrave Macmillan Ltd. Macmillan® is a registered trademark in the United States, United Kingdom and other countries. Palgrave is a registered trademark in the European Union and other countries.

ISBN 1-4039-6377-0 hardback

Library of Congress Cataloging-in-Publication Data

Banks, Erik.
    Working the Street : what you need to know about life on Wall Street / by Erik Banks.
        p. cm.
    Includes bibliographical references and index.
    ISBN 1-4039-6377-0
    1. Stockbrokers—United States. 2. Wall Street. I. Title.

    HG4928.5.B36 2004
    332.6'2—dc21

                                                                        2003054933

A catalogue record for this book is available from the British Library.

Design by Planettheo.com.

First edition: February 2004
10 9 8 7 6 5 4 3 2 1

Printed in the United States of America.

CONTENTS

ACKNOWLEDGMENTS

I would like to thank Toby Wahl, senior editor at Palgrave Macmillan in New York, for his invaluable support and advice on this project. Thanks are also due to Donna Cherry and the production and marketing teams at Palgrave for their assistance in creating the book. Sincere thanks also go to the many Wall Streeters I have had the privilege of working with over the years—they taught me, gave me opportunities, and made the whole experience fun.

And my biggest thanks go, of course, to my wife, Milena!

—EB
Redding, Connecticut, 2003
Ebbrisk@netscape.net

BIO

Erik Banks spent sixteen years on Wall Street, most of it at a major global investment bank. After training and early job experience in New York, he spent eight years running departments in Tokyo, Hong Kong, and London, and then returned to New York as a managing director. Mr. Banks retired from Wall Street in 2002 to write full time; he is the author of a dozen books on banking, risk, derivatives, and governance.

PREFACE

Wall Street is a place of *extremes:* good markets and bad, great deals and bombs, fantastic people and horrible ones. These extremes—the booms and busts, the good and bad—help define Wall Street and give it its character and flavor. The booms are fun, exciting, and lucrative. The busts are painful and sometimes financially and personally devastating—but a tremendous proving ground.

Wall Street also occupies a *unique reality.* What happens on The Street is so quirky—sometimes even bizarre—that no analogue exists. There simply aren't any other markets, industries, companies, or businesses that can give you an idea of what Wall Street is all about: compensation has no grounding in reality, the responsibilities that are given to young people are without parallel, the excesses that occasionally pile up are astounding, and the business that gets done is truly spectacular.

The extremes and the unique reality make it challenging to describe what Wall Street is really all about. If you haven't lived it for a while it is tough explaining it in a way that actually makes sense and still seems believable—though that is what this book will try to do.

I feel fortunate to have been part of Wall Street for so many years. And I feel especially lucky that my tenure spanned important, exciting, and wrenching times—actually, some of the most intense in the history of the business world. From the time I arrived as a completely green but very eager banker-in-training in 1986 until the day I left in 2002, Wall Street went through absolutely tremendous peaks and troughs: the Latin debt crisis, the U.S. savings and loan crisis, the rise and fall (and subsequent resurrection) of junk bonds and corporate takeovers, the decade-long global stock market bull run, the bursting of Japan's enormous economic bubble, the pulverization of several high-flying Asian and Latin economies, the collapse of some big hedge funds, the unreal Internet and technology boom and bust, the corporate accounting scandals and government privatizations, the implosion of communism, the wars, the peace, and everything in between. These cycles were my education. As the saying goes, "Everyone's a hero in a bull market"—but it takes the bear markets, the nasty dislocations, bankruptcies, scandals, losses, and failures to really teach you something. And if scars, bruises, nicks, and cuts are the measure, I've learned a lot from my time on Wall Street. I had the chance to work during screaming bull markets when money poured into Wall Street, and dark, dark, dark hours when recovery seemed an impossibility. I had the chance to work with some great, inspired teachers, and I had the misfortune of coming across some real bad apples.

So this book is my view on how it all works. My pet peeves and biases probably shine through on occasion, but I suppose that's the point. I haven't had to color anything, though—*Wall Street is what it is*, for better or worse.

So, for those of you starting out on Wall Street, those of you switching gears and jumping into the deep end, or those of you already in the thick of things, I hope this book gives you a bit more flavor about what working The Street is like.

Working The Street

CHAPTER ONE

Middleman:
What Wall Street Really Does

WHY WORK ON WALL STREET?

Most of us work because we want to and we need to. We want to do something where we can learn, contribute, interact socially and have some fun, and we need to keep our minds challenged. Can you imagine what it would be like to sit around doing nothing all the time? Since we have to spend so much of our time on the job—40, 50, or 60 hours a week, maybe even more—we'd better enjoy what we're doing.

And, let's face it, we need, and we want, the cash.

We need to pay for the rent, food, electricity, and to set aside something for retirement. And we want all the things that make life a bit more comfortable and exciting: a nice car, maybe a Caribbean vacation, the latest electronic gear.

Unfortunately, there just aren't many places where you can work hard, have fun, and get paid well—all at the same time. So when, or if, you find such a place, you would be foolish not to at least consider it.

Happily, there is Wall Street: the hub of the machinery that keeps the global economic wheels turning. A place where you can be at the center of the action, have a good time, and keep mentally sharp while earning a more than fair share of the American Dream.

Yes, Wall Street is aggressive and occasionally pushes the edge of the envelope. It shoots itself in the foot every so often, and it goes through ferocious bloodlettings every few years. It's not an easy place to work if you are thin-skinned, faint of heart, or prone to nervous stress. You need lots of stamina, some political savvy, and a reasonable amount of intelligence. And you have to be singularly focused, energized, and dedicated. But if you've got these traits and skills and can get in the door and prove yourself, the chances are you will have fun and do very well.

Sure, you could always work somewhere else, but then you'd be compromising instead of maximizing. You could be a management consultant and probably be intellectually stimulated—but not get paid much. You could be an e-commerce or technology entrepreneur, but you risk blowing up and having to start all over again. You could be a venture capitalist and get paid well if you do well, but get dumped quickly if you back the wrong horse. Or you could be a doctor, lawyer, accountant, or corporate middle manager. But why?

Only Wall Street delivers the unique combination of intellectual stimulation, excitement, and compensation. If that's what you're looking for, this is the place for you.

So, what is this book all about? Well, let's start with what it is not: it is not a how-to career book or a job guide. It doesn't list the people you need to contact to advise you on what classes to take to prepare for your career or tell you what kind of prior job experience you need in order to make it. And it is not a book about the technical nuts and bolts of Wall Street; it won't tell you what stocks and bonds to buy, or how inflation and taxes affect the economy, or the differences between 401(k)s and IRAs. Some really good books are already out there that talk about all of that.

This book is a bit different. It's about some of the ins and outs of working on Wall Street, about how things really work in the financial world, about some of the speed bumps you should watch out for, and the low-hanging fruit that is ripe for the picking. It's about tricks that will make your career a bit easier and about situations you should avoid if you want to survive.

If you want to have fun and make some dollars, if you want to work hard at something interesting so you can eventually enjoy life on your own terms—if you want to work on Wall Street—then you need to know as much as you can about how it really operates.

WHAT DOES WALL STREET REALLY DO?

If you are thinking about a Wall Street career—maybe you are finishing your undergraduate degree or MBA, or already working somewhere else but thinking about switching jobs—you may have some vague idea about what happens on the lower tip of Manhattan, but everything you know comes from books, movies, or TV, not from real life. And your parents, spouse, or kids, no matter how smart, probably don't have a clue about what Wall Street does, either. So let's set the record straight.

To the uninitiated there is something mysterious and scary about Wall Street, about screaming traders and vast quantities of money flying around the world through computers, about big financial deals, and mergers and acquisitions (M&A), and hostile takeovers. Lots of people are afraid of this, because it looks and sounds intimidating, and there are large amounts of money involved. If it involves a lot of money, it has to be complicated, right?

Have you ever watched the evening business news and seen all of those people in yellow jackets, packed shoulder-to-shoulder on the floor of some exchange, screaming and waving at each other, faces red and purple—looking either absolutely elated or wildly panicked? Do you remember the movie *Wall Street*—all the money changing hands, the "greed is good" speech, the little companies buying the big ones, the "inside information" circulating between good guys and bad guys, the eight-panel cutaway shot of the trading floors with high-powered executives earning and losing millions? For many of you, these TV and movie scenes represent Wall Street—and they make it seem so complicated and unintelligible.

In reality, Wall Street isn't very complicated at all. When you peel back the layers, the financial world that emerges is surprisingly simple. People have been doing this stuff for centuries. True, the dollars are bigger, the computers faster, and the jargon a bit snappier, but in the end it's all pretty elemental. Wall Street just prefers to shroud itself in a bit of mystery, some unnecessary opacity. Preserving the mystique, the illusion of complexity, is very important—it provides a measure of self-importance (and helps justify large paychecks).

Sending a man to the moon is complicated. Building science and engineering marvels—like the Channel Tunnel, or the newest, tiniest, fastest microchip—is complicated. Wall Street is not. Some Wall Streeters will surely protest when they read this, but they are wrong. You can forgive them: they are just part of the group that likes to perpetuate the myth that Wall Street is a special place with special people, an exclusive club consisting of members who have capabilities and intellect that most people just don't have. (And paying these club members astronomical sums helps reinforce the attitude and behavior. The equation is simple: one, two, or three extra zeros on a paycheck signifies a "very important person" with special knowledge—which means that it's all too complicated for regular people to understand.)

So let's dispel the myth of complexity by looking at what Wall Street really does.

Wall Street is a middleman—actually, the consummate middleman—that performs five functions, usually very well (of course, it does many smaller things as well, but they all revolve around five basic ones). So, as a middleman does, it takes a cut of the action whenever it can (through fees, and lots of them, which helps when bonus season comes around).

Function #1:
Raising Money for People, Companies and Countries

People, companies, and countries need to borrow money. They may want to make a big purchase, say a flat-screen TV or a factory, or make an emergency payment to the plumber if the pipes burst, or to the computer company if the network goes down. Whatever the reason, Wall Street is always ready to get money to those who need it, for a fee (kind of like a loan shark). Investment bankers and traders (whom we'll meet later in the book) usually handle this task.

You basically have three choices when it comes to getting money: a loan, a bond, or a stock. You already know what a loan is; you've probably borrowed at some point in your life. You go to your bank, fill out some loan forms, put up some kind of an asset as security (probably your house or car), and get the money, which you repay with interest over time. Wall Street makes loans not just to people but to companies and countries. Really good companies or countries don't have to put up any assets as security, but bad ones do, because there is always a chance that they won't be able to make good on their loans when they're supposed to. If the loans don't get repaid, Wall Street just sells the security and repays itself (kind of like a pawnbroker).

Wall Street can also raise money through a bond—it usually does this for companies and countries rather than for people. A bond is really just an IOU with more legal language attached: it says that the bank will give you $100 in exchange for your promise to repay the $100, plus interest, in the future. It's kind of like a loan, but the IOU can actually be sold to someone else (see Function #2). Companies and countries issue lots of IOUs every day to raise cash.

As a company you can also raise money by selling stock—sort of a permanent loan that never has to be repaid. Again, you probably know what a share of stock is because you almost certainly have a few in your retirement plan or through your local investment club. But what does a share of stock really represent? It's actually a small piece of a company. If you have a share of IBM stock, you own a very, very, very small piece of IBM. In exchange, you have given IBM your money as a kind of permanent loan. Instead of getting paid interest for lending IBM the money, you may get a dividend payment every quarter—and you'll get some extra money if the price of IBM goes up when you sell your share. If you decide you want your money back, you don't ask IBM to repay you; you just sell your IBM share to someone else who wants to buy it (see Function #2). You get your money back, and the new buyer steps into your shoes.

Raising money for people and companies and countries has been happening for a long time. The Bank of Venice started lending money in the twelfth century, and Jewish moneylenders were doing the same thing in London's Cheapside, Old Jewry, and Lombard Street a century later. So it isn't anything particularly new.

Function #2:
Buying and Selling Stocks and Bonds and Other Things

Wall Street is really good at buying and selling just about anything. That's not too surprising, since that's what middlemen usually do. In fact, Wall Street is a giant marketplace for exchanging almost any item with a dollar value. All the buying and selling happens through traders and salespeople (whom we'll also meet in due course).

Wall Street buys and sells things we all know about, like stocks, bonds (IOUs), currencies, oil, gold, gas, coffee, pork bellies, feeder cattle, and frozen concentrated orange juice. It also buys and sells things that are a bit more esoteric, like palladium, benzene, sunflower seeds, soybean meal, electricity, and freight. And sometimes it buys and sells things that are just strange, like temperature (yes, it's true), catastrophe, microchips, inflation, financial volatility, bankruptcy, and Internet bandwidth; and it even buys and sells the difference *between* things, rather than the things themselves— like the difference between oil and gasoline (a "crack spread") or electricity and natural gas (a "spark spread"). So it doesn't really matter what is involved, as long as there is some value to it. Then the blueprint is really simple: buy low and sell high, or borrow, sell high, rebuy low, and repay.

Wall Street buys and sells in two ways: as a dealer, it buys from you at $100 and sells to me at $105 (taking the $5 for itself), or as an agent, it matches you and me up at $102.50 and then steps out of the way (after collecting a fee). Wall Street usually acts as a dealer, buying something on the cheap, and then trying to sell it for more, kind of like a used-car dealer. It's a bit riskier than being an agent, because the price may fall before the sale. But Wall Streeters love a bit of risk because there's always a chance to earn more money.

None of this, of course, is new. People have been buying and selling things for quite a few centuries, ever since money became an accepted medium of exchange (before that it was just bartering, exchanging goods for goods). Now they just buy and sell different things: instead of buying conch shells (or olive oil or papyrus scrolls) at $100 and selling them at $105, they buy a share of IBM at $100 and sell it at $105. Same idea, though.

Function #3:
Telling Companies and Countries What to Do
with Their Money

People like to give advice. It's human nature: parents to kids ("do your homework"), wives to husbands ("cut the grass"), bosses to subordinates ("get me some coffee"). Wall Street is no different: it likes to tell companies and countries what to do (very politely, of course). But unlike the free advice you and I give or get, Wall Street, as middleman, charges a fee, kind of like a psychiatrist.

Companies and countries have to grow in order to get ahead and to stay ahead. They have to come up with new products, get into new markets, buy up competitors, build new highways and hospitals, or sell off their national treasures (such as wireless spectrum or oil fields). Wall Streeters—investment bankers, specifically—are always ready to help them out by thinking up ideas that they hope will leave the competition (that is, the company or country next door) in the dust. They scan the horizon for opportunities that seem sensible, do lots of number crunching and analysis, make slick presentations to CEOs and finance ministers and try to convince them that their ideas are good. If the powers-that-be like an idea, they may engage the Wall Street crew to "make it so," for a fee. If they don't like the idea, they tell the Wall Streeters to go away, for a fee. Sometimes a Wall Street house may even advise a company or country to undo the advice given to it by some other Wall Street house a few years back, for a fee.

It will come to you as no surprise that this business has been going on for a long time as well: bankers have been advising companies and countries to buy things (such as the Suez Canal) or create things (such as steel and railroad cartels) for several hundred years, even lending them the money to do it (Function #1). Nothing new.

Function #4:
Telling People What to Do with Their Money

The last distinct thing that Wall Street does, and the most important for many, is telling men and women on Main Street what to do with their money. This usually happens through retail salespeople (though many now prefer to be called financial advisors or wealth consultants). It's just like Function #3, but on a more personal level.

People need to do something with their money: save it and invest it so that they have enough for a new car, a new house, their kid's schooling (including business school so that some new Wall Streeters can be minted), and retirement. So Wall Street has specialists that advise people on what they should do with their salary and assets: how much they should save every year and how much they should put in stocks or bonds in order to meet their financial goals. They also talk about really boring—but really important—things like retirement plans, tax and estate planning, and insurance. Kind of like a guidance counselor. Naturally, all of this advice is useful, so it costs money, more fees. In fact, many people pay for an initial consultation (an "introductory" fee), the ongoing advice (an annual "wealth management" fee) and individual transactions (commissions or "transaction" fees). And—you've guessed it—none of this is new. It's been happening for a long time.

Function #5:
Functions #1, #2, #3, and #4 . . . All at Once

Wall Street sometimes gets to link Functions #1, #2, #3, and #4 together—this is known as "firing on all cylinders," which brings in lots of fees. The cycle goes like this:

- Wall Street bank A advises company B to buy one of its competitors (Function #3, for which it earns a fee).
- Company B agrees, but it doesn't have enough money, so Wall Street bank A offers to issue a bond (IOU) for company B (Function #1, for a fee).
- It then advises personal client C of a good investment opportunity in this new bond (IOU) (Function #4, fee!).
- It then sells the bond (IOU) to personal client C (Function #2, fee!!).
- Of course, if, a few weeks, months, or years from now, personal client C wants to get rid of the bond (IOU) because it needs some extra cash or wants to invest in something else, Wall Street bank A will buy it back (Function #2 again, fee!!!). Cool, isn't it?

So that is really all that Wall Street is, and does—part loan shark, part pawnbroker, part used-car dealer, part psychiatrist, part guidance counselor. And it just replicates practices that have existed, in some form, for the past few centuries.

Of course, not every firm on Wall Street does every one of these things all the time. Some Wall Street firms are niche players or "boutiques"—very specialized, focused on, for example, giving advice to companies or individuals, or trading, or raising money. Other firms are like big financial supermarkets—"all things to all people"—and do a bit (or a lot) of everything. A few years ago firms that lent money weren't allowed to issue and trade stocks or bonds—but that's all changed now, so a firm can be a big supermarket if it wants to be.

Now you can see that what Wall Street actually does is pretty simple. But, remember—even though it's not terribly complicated, it *is* very hard work. Wall Street works hard and demands hard work. And as we've noted, it's aggressive and political. But the payoff is in the fun, the challenge, and the excitement, and in the possibility of earning lots of money (enough, as we'll see, for early retirement).

So if you think you are interested in playing in this arena, read on—let's see if there's any surefire way of landing a Wall Street job.

CHAPTER TWO

Entrance, Stage Right: Getting in the Door

How many times have you heard someone say: "I'm better than that guy. I could do what he's doing—ten times better and ten times faster. If I could just get in the door, I'd show them what a great job I could do."

Not only have you heard people say it, you've probably said it yourself (or are actually saying it). And, even though you know you could really dazzle them if you could get in the door, how do you actually get in the door? What does Wall Street want, what is it looking for? What is the secret formula for landing a job so that you can start delivering the goods?

THERE IS NO SECRET FORMULA

At the risk of starting off on a sour note, the truth is that there is *no* secret formula for getting on The Street. There just isn't a neat little equation, like:

Great Resume +
Good Degree(s) +
Relevant Work Experience +
Chairman's Son's Golf Buddy +
Charming, Good-Looking, Witty =
Guaranteed Job on Wall Street

After you've spent a bit of time on Wall Street you'll be convinced of this fact because you'll see that just about anything can, and does, happen. You'll see folks with Ivy League MBAs who can't get in the door no matter how hard they try and state school liberal arts majors who seem to breeze right in (and vice versa). You'll see folks with lots of experience get turned away, and fresh graduate recruits welcomed with open arms (and vice versa). You'll see folks who have no contacts somehow make it through the door, and networkers who know everyone fail to even line up an interview (and vice versa). Anything goes.

So, you'll see everything—meaning that anything is possible, and that no prescribed formula applies (unless you are shooting for one of the very senior executive management slots on The Street—there pedigree and connections matter a lot. More on this later).

But why isn't there a formula? Why isn't there a template that you can follow that will guarantee you access? Probably because Wall Street is the kind of place that lets people prove themselves. Wall Street knows, from years of experience, that people from virtually any background, any walk of life, can get in and excel . . . so why should it limit itself by creating an artificial template—one that says The Street will only accept candidates from these schools, or with this experience or that background? Every firm, every situation, every market cycle, every job, and every candidate is unique, so a "cookie cutter" approach just doesn't work. Again, a bit of time on The Street will convince you that all kinds of people can succeed— just as all kinds can fail. You'll see new graduates land entry-level analyst jobs and do well, and others blow up after just six months. You'll see experienced lawyers move to The Street and hit their stride, just as some of their JD colleagues give up and run back to the sanctuary of some corporate law office. You'll see superintelligent academics get in and revamp a research area, and others just collapse. You'll see technologists, with no accounting or finance background, shift gears and become solid bankers, and high school graduates, starting off as operations clerks, become great traders. Anything goes.

So, any combination of skills and background can actually be put to good use on Wall Street. And this means that as you set off on your Wall Street quest, you've got to be ready to use whatever you have, whatever you know, and whoever you know to try and get in. Because anything goes.

MBA: NICE TO HAVE,
BUT DEFINITELY NOT NECESSARY

Now that we've captured the attention of every bleary-eyed, debt-laden MBA student seeking to further his or her career, let's dig into this a bit deeper. We don't mean that if you want to work on Wall Street you can't or shouldn't have an MBA—we mean that if you don't have one, don't want one or can't get one, you'll still be able to succeed on The Street.

Let's face it, for the right person an MBA can be a useful experience and a good prejob "training platform" (if you're a liberal arts undergrad and decide to get your MBA to learn more about the business world, then you'll probably learn a few useful things along the way). And Wall Street still hires lots of MBAs—that's the focus of The Street's recruiting efforts, and its payoff has generally been good, so why change it? That means if you've got an MBA, or are trying to get one, your chances of seeing a few Wall Street recruiters on campus increase.

But non-MBAs should take heart. Things have loosened up a bit, and Wall Street managers and human resource specialists have started realizing that they actually miss the best cross section of human experience if they hire only business majors—lots of very successful and talented Wall Streeters don't even have business degrees. So now they're recruiting liberal arts folks, math and science majors, law graduates. Wall Street has discovered that sometimes it's better to have a creative, enthusiastic history or English major or a hard-core math, science, or law major: someone well-rounded who can think about things in a new light or a specialist who knows some important, and sometimes complicated, things in great detail. Who knows, maybe Wall Street would be a better place if it had a few more people who knew about the lessons of history, about what the French naturalists or English Victorians said, about ethics and psychology, or about foreign culture and language.

At the analyst or associate level—the entry-level jobs that we'll get into in the next chapter—the most important qualifications are enthusiasm and a complete willingness to sacrifice your personal life for the greater good of the company. The specific business skills required—like the ones you're supposed to learn in B-school—are actually taught (or retaught, in a useful and practical way) in the training program and on the job. If you've already been working in some other field, you probably bring enough job skills to the table without an MBA; recruiters are talking to you because of your professional knowledge, not your classroom knowledge, so the most important things are hands-on experience, contacts, and maturity—not whether you took accounting 400 and marketing 401, or excelled at case studies.

So if you're thinking about getting an MBA and know *exactly* why you want it (not just to "open doors," but to actually teach you something you don't know or can't learn in some other way), go ahead. If you're halfway through your program, finish it. But if you don't have an MBA and want to work on The Street, don't be discouraged—lack of an MBA doesn't mean that you can't do the job or won't be considered for the job. On the contrary: if you've got intelligence, energy, and dedication—and can prove it—you don't need the three "magic letters" to make you successful.

KNOW WHY YOU WANT TO BE ON WALL STREET

Before you start the task at hand—the process of trying to land a job on Wall Street—it's a good idea to take a step back and understand exactly why you want to be a Wall Streeter. What is it that appeals to you about Wall Street, and why do you want to be there? Is it the money? Is it because you are interested in banking? Is it because you're attracted to the pace, excitement, and energy? Is it because you think your personality is perfectly suited for an intense and relentless work environment? Is it because you like to work hard and play hard? Is it because you believe that Wall Street actually has important and meaningful work to do in helping investors and clients? Is it some of these, all of these, none of these? Is it something else?

Going through this process is important because if you know, and can justify, exactly why you want to work on Wall Street—in a logical, well-articulated way—you'll be able to convince others. You'll be able to express—with confidence, certainty, and poise—exactly why you belong on Wall Street, and that conviction will shine through when you're going to interviews and getting grilled by recruiters. It'll help convince them that you've thought it through and know how and why you'll make a difference.

So spend some time thinking about your reasons for wanting to be on The Street before you plunge in. But a word of caution: never think, or say, that you are in it only for the money. That's perfectly okay as part of the larger picture, but if you come across as a hired-gun/mercenary type, you're not going to get far. The compensation aspect is already well understood—by you, the recruiters, the firms—so you don't have to be obvious about it.

MAKE SURE YOU'RE READY FOR WALL STREET

It's not enough for you to know *why* you want to be on Wall Street—you've got to make sure that you're *physically* and *mentally* ready to be there. We've already said that Wall Street is brutal. It demands energy, focus, dedication, and a wholehearted willingness to sacrifice. It also requires stamina. The work that you do on The Street—the intense pace you've got to maintain and the daily pressures that you'll be exposed to—last for years and years (until retirement day, actually).

In moving on to The Street, you'll need to give up lots of things—either temporarily or permanently—that are fun and interesting. Your personal life—hobbies, friends, and even family—will have to take a back seat to your job, your sleep patterns will be completely altered, your vacation and weekend time will never really be your own. It'll be difficult to relax, to put your guard down. Since your life will be exposed to this relentless pummeling for many years to come, make sure you're really ready for it. There's no point taking a shot at The Street if you're not ready to give it 100 percent of your physical and mental attention, all the time.

CLIFF DWELLERS GET PAID MORE FOR A REASON

As you think about all of the reasons why you want to be on Wall Street, you've got to think about this one long and hard:

If you are going to take more risk, you are going to want more return.
If you are going to take less risk, you should expect less return.

Putting this in the context of a Wall Street job:

risk = lack of job security
return = year-end compensation.

One obvious reason you want to be on Wall Street (the one you're not supposed to blurt out during the interviews) is because you want to earn money. A lot more than your neighbors, a lot more than your business school professors, a lot more than doctors, lawyers, and accountants (and, actually, a lot more than folks at the venture capital/management consultant/e-commerce firms that occasionally think they will best Wall Street for all the talent). And if you decide to accept a Wall Street job and that handsome paycheck (return) you've got to remember that you are also accepting a much greater chance of losing your job (risk). That's the trade-off. You will be living on the edge of a cliff—and it's a long way down if you happen to slide off.

As economists like to say, there is no free lunch. If you can't handle the prospect of getting fired for any reason (or, on Wall Street, for no reason at all), then you shouldn't be willing to accept the large paycheck—and you probably shouldn't be looking for a job on The Street. If you want a safe and comfortable job where there is zero risk of getting fired, become a government employee, a local CPA, or a high school teacher. Nine to five, three weeks of vacation every year, modest salary and benefits, a fruitcake as your year-end bonus, and no job-loss worries—no chance for a home-run payday either, but that's the trade-off.

Of course, you'll find that even on Wall Street there are varying levels of job security, which we'll talk more about later in the book. For now, though, think through very carefully if you can handle the prospect of living on the edge of the cliff. If you can, then move ahead, carefully. If not, then just stay on safe ground and let others sit close to the edge.

FORGET YOUR PRIDE—USE ALL YOUR CONTACTS

The interviewing process is obviously the starting point in trying to land a job. You are going up against lots of people who are trying to chase the same Wall Street dream, so the competition is ridiculously stiff. That means you've got to swallow your pride, and dig out any contact or connection that you think might lead to Wall Street—no matter how uncomfortable it might be or how much of a long shot it might seem. You just never know.

Don't just rely on college placement offices, or headhunters, or executive recruiters, or newspaper ads, or your personal/family connections, or internships, or friends, or sorority sisters, or racquetball partners, or whomever. Rely on all of them, simultaneously. Your odds of landing on The Street will increase significantly. Ask anyone and everyone who might know someone who's already working on The Street to get your résumé to the right person, to arrange a quick "informational chat" over coffee, to put in an introductory phone call or send them a brief e-mail—anything that will help get you noticed, so that you don't wind up in the dreaded "stack of unsolicited résumés" that sits on the desk of every busy Wall Streeter, gathering dust.

And remember that tapping into your network will entail a little quid pro quo later on—Wall Street relies on favors to get things done. So, if someone does you a favor by setting up an interview and it eventually leads somewhere, you can bet you will be asked to repay it. There is no charity on Wall Street.

A LITTLE CREATIVITY, PLEASE

If you find some contacts who are willing to look at your credentials or who can get them to the right people on The Street, don't blow the opportunity with a bad résumé. And don't blow it with something that's even worse than bad: a boring résumé.

Most people's résumés are, for the lack of a better word, dull. Most come straight out of career and résumé guidebooks, or from the style sheets given out by college placement offices, and are so scripted and uniform that they're unpleasant to read—so they tend not to get read. Most say the same thing: this is my objective, these are my relevant courses, internships, and past jobs, these are the computer operating systems I am familiar with, and this is the year I studied abroad and this is . . . what a snooze.

Of course the firm and its recruiters need to know all that stuff—eventually. But in order to get noticed, to distinguish yourself, try delivering something different, creative, eye-catching. Shake it up a little, because Wall Street is actually a fun place— it's not all deals and numbers and sales and trades. It's about doing things in a new, exciting, and pioneering way. So if you can show some of that creativity on your résumé—a little thinking outside of the box—you'll at least distinguish yourself from the hordes that use the frightful "résumé template." Fundamentally, it all comes down to marketing. You're not going to buy the newest Compaq laptop (or Nike running shoes or Mercedes SUV) if you don't know about it—and you'll know about it only if something in the marketing catches your eye. The same applies to you. A Wall Street firm isn't going to hire you unless it knows you exist, and it won't know you exist if you follow the same dull path. If you can show the firm you're out there by marketing yourself through a creative résumé, you've got a much better chance of getting in the door for an interview.

Imagine that two otherwise identical and qualified candidates deliver their resumes: one indicates that she's taken Principles of Corporate Finance and Advanced Cost Accounting, has done a semester abroad at the Sorbonne to improve her conversational French, and is president of the local chapter of the accounting club; the other indicates that she just completed a research paper showing Keynes had it all wrong, that her particular hobby is determining how Trollope's mid-nineteenth century novels can give us all lessons on improving corporate governance, that she trains rescue dogs in her free time, and that she has run the Sahara ultramarathon. Who's going to get the first (and maybe only) call to come in for a chat? Think about it, and try to make a difference when presenting yourself.

LEAVE YOUR ATTITUDE AT HOME

Once you've managed to interest someone in your background—by tapping your contacts and showing them something creative—you'll be set for your interviews. This is obviously where you get to make a real face-to-face impression—and the result will depend almost entirely on how you handle yourself. This is "make-or-break" time. If you want to work on Wall Street, you can't screw this up. And remember, as you're getting yourself psyched up, to leave your attitude at home. There just isn't any room for attitude during the interview process. What exactly do we mean by attitude? Lack of respect, arrogance, pride, boastfulness, impatience, anything that will cause your interviewer to turn ice cold and shuffle you out the door.

Don't try to impress whoever interviews you, whether a human resource specialist, an investment banker, or a sales manager. Most of them have seen it all, and heard it all, before. Don't try to snow anyone with your "expert" knowledge of bond convexity or poison pill defenses or dual class recapitalizations or cash flow analysis techniques—unless you are specifically asked to. (Since you don't really know what they really know, just play it safe. More than a few candidates have gone down in flames by speaking too freely on subjects that they didn't really know as well as they thought they did.) And never talk down to anyone, even when it's obvious that you're smarter—treat people with respect, regardless of their job, intellect, or seniority (remember, they work on Wall Street already, you don't).

Just present yourself the way you are. Tell your interviewers honestly, and convincingly, why you want to work on The Street, about your skills and how they are relevant. Be humble, patient, enthusiastic, speak when you are spoken to, and if that's not how you normally are, then just pretend for a while. You've worked hard to get yourself wedged in the door, so don't do anything silly to jeopardize your chances.

SHOW SOME INTEREST

After all the trouble you've taken preparing your credentials, setting up interviews through your contact network and getting pumped up for the big day(s), don't stumble by not knowing something about Wall Street and the firm you are visiting.

Take the time to do some research. If you come in knowing something about the people you're talking to, you're just proving that you care—that you've put in the time to learn about the firm and are genuinely interested in being there and possibly working there. You aren't wasting the company's time or your time. It's easy to tell when a candidate is prepared and when one isn't.

So how do you prepare, what should you know? Know about the company, its businesses, strategic initiatives, growth and contraction areas, financial strengths, potential weaknesses, how it stacks up against the competition, where it ranks in different business lines, how it reacts in different market conditions and cycles, how it's perceived in the marketplace, what the stock price has been doing, and what the debt and equity analysts are saying. And know how you can fit into all of this. That demonstrates that you are linking your own capabilities and views to what the firm is trying to get done. Most of this information is publicly available, so do some legwork, run your Google search, get hold of the facts, form your strategy and questions, and let the recruiter know (during the right moments) what you know. Your interest will be noticed and noted.

If you've gotten this far, don't blow it by being sloppy. It seems so elemental, but it's amazing how often candidates show up on Wall Street utterly clueless about the firm and the industry. It looks bad, and it's a surefire way of not being asked back for more interviews. So be prepared.

THERE IS NOTHING WRONG WITH THE BACK DOOR

Sometimes you just can't get in the front door, no matter what you do. You may have an interesting résumé, a few contacts, and do well on the interviews, but it may not be quite enough. Let's say you desperately want to be part of the analyst program so that you can become a junior trader and work your way up the ranks. You do well during interviews, but the analyst program is full for the year or your skills don't match up with what the firm wants at that exact moment. That will seem unfair after all your hard work—but don't give up. Try the back door.

Take a shot at some other job at the firm—maybe a back-office function, a technology job, or one of the supposedly less glamorous (but, frankly, no less important) jobs. If your goal is really to get onto Wall Street to be a trader (or whatever), don't be shy about taking a different, nontraditional, route—whatever it takes to get in the door, to get a Wall Street job. Because once you're in the door, in whatever position, you'll be noticed if you are good, diligent, and hardworking. You'll have a chance to get to know the right people and will ultimately be able to make an internal move. Remember that a firm favors its own. If it knows of a qualified candidate within its four walls that can fill a job opening (on the trading floor, for instance), it'll take that person rather than search externally—so the odds are in your favor once you're in the door.

In the meantime, if you are doing your less than ideal job as a first step in your career, use it to your advantage. Learn everything you can, meet everyone you can, and make the best of the situation. Take the long view and be patient. You're building a career on Wall Street, so whether you are working in your ideal trading job now, next year or in three years shouldn't matter that much. But remember—whatever you are doing, you've got to do it well, and with enthusiasm. Just because it isn't what you were expecting to do doesn't mean you shouldn't give it 100 percent. You are on Wall Street and you want to stay there so that you can advance to "greener pastures." If you slack off, you are out—so don't slack off. There is no shame in doing an honest day's work in a second-choice job if it will eventually lead you where you want to go.

LUCK MATTERS,
SO KEEP TRYING UNTIL SOME COMES YOUR WAY

Let's face it, luck matters in everything we do—sometimes that seems unfair, but that's life. Some people think we make our own luck—well, maybe we do, maybe not. That's in the realm of the metaphysical, and we don't need to go there. One thing is certain: luck, in whatever form it takes, matters when you are trying to land a job on The Street. All of the stars have to align properly for you to get that "dream job." You've got to be in the right place at the right time, talking to the right person and connecting on some level, convincing that person that you've got the right skills—and the firm has to be looking for your skill set at that exact moment. When you stop and think about all of these moving parts, it'll seem like the odds are stacked against you—and sometimes they are.

So if luck favors you and helps get you in the door, great. If it doesn't, don't beat yourself up, don't take it personally and definitely don't stop trying—especially if you've decided that Wall Street is where you really want to be. Just keep trying, because sooner or later luck will favor you. If you've got the desire and perseverance and energy, keep at it, and a little luck will help make it happen.

ONCE YOU'RE IN, FORGET WHAT YOU KNOW

If you've made it through the process—good interviews, good chemistry, good match of skills and interests—you'll get an offer letter, and you'll be on your way to Wall Street. Congratulations! All of your hard work and tenacity has paid off (and in the midst of your jubilation, don't forget to thank all of those who helped get you there).

But as you are preparing for your first day at the firm—whether you're a recent graduate or someone who's been around the working world for a bit—remember this: you've got to forget everything you know. That will irritate some of you—particularly if you pride yourself on your educational background, your knowledge, your past work experiences. Isn't that why you got hired? Partly, but it was mostly for your potential, your enthusiasm, and your perceived ability to contribute.

Wall Street is funny. It wants to teach you things the "Wall Street way"—a way that's unique, very different from school or from other industries (we'll see just how different in the next few chapters). And since each individual firm on Wall Street is special in some way, each one wants to teach you what you need to know in a way that makes sense for its business operations. That doesn't mean you should forget the basics—that bond prices fall when interest rates go up or that assets minus liabilities equal equity. Just don't think that everything you learned as an undergrad or in B-school, or on the job at the local community bank, applies. So just empty your mind, became mentally open and flexible. It will help prepare you for the little bit of agony that follows—the brainwashing boot-camp experience in which your mind gets stuffed with all kinds of things the firm really wants you to know.

CHAPTER THREE

Paying Your Dues:
The Life of Trainees, Analysts, and Associates

So you made it through all of the interviews, have your new job all lined up, and bought a new wardrobe and briefcase. You are ready to show the world what you've got. Good.

But wait. Unless you're filling an existing job as an experienced hire, you're actually not quite ready to show the world what you've got. Before you get to run with the big dogs, before you can start digging into all the fun and interesting stuff that Wall Street has to offer—working on mega-deals, landing new clients, circling the globe in search of business—you'll have to go through a period of very intense training and education, a sort of hazing process (though one where you actually get paid) that teaches you Wall Street's ways. Only when you complete this training and education will you have a shot at a permanent job somewhere in the firm. Until then, you should consider yourself "stateless."

In short, you have to "pay your dues." Paying your dues is a way of giving you experience and credibility, of showing you how things get done on Wall Street. And it's a way of letting the firm separate the wheat from the chaff, to find out if you (and your new colleagues) really belong on The

Street. Paying your dues—as a trainee and then an analyst—means living through a kind of hellish existence that lasts anywhere from three to five years, a hell from which you will emerge a semi-hardened, slightly jaded Wall Streeter. Assuming you emerge.

START AT GO: TRAINING

If you are an undergraduate, or have an advanced degree but no Wall Street experience, you'll be assigned to the training program as a trainee (aka "the lowest of the low") on your first day of work. If you've got a few years of experience under your belt, consider yourself fortunate—you get to skip ahead.

This part of your career is kind of like joining the Marine Corps as an enlisted soldier, and going off to boot camp for basic training. Instead of climbing over walls, crawling under barbed wire, running 10 miles in the rain, doing lots of push-ups and shooting at live targets, you:

- Go to classes all day long and learn about the essential of corporate finance, financial math, international economics, mergers and acquisitions, traded markets, and securities settlements (and how to use an HP12-C financial calculator . . . yep, they still use them).
- Get together with your fellow trainees in the evenings to work on problem sets, case studies and mock presentations. (Sleep tends to be the sacrificial lamb at this point.)
- Make deal presentations and sales pitches in front of all of your colleagues and instructors, an occasion for you to get grilled, challenged, ripped to shreds, and humiliated.
- Take quizzes and tests, mostly without advance warning.
- Repeat the same schedule all week (and on weekends if you want to stay a bit ahead of the curve), week after week, month after month, for six months to a year, depending on the firm.

And you have to do all of this really well. You get graded and evaluated all along the way, so you can't afford to mess up. The bottom 10 percent or 20 percent or 30 percent (depending on the firm and the state of the markets) gets dropped—and you don't want to get dropped.

So it's probably more painful than boot camp. That's why we said in that last chapter that you should forget what you know—it'll make the indoctrination process easier. The sponge that has been wrung dry can absorb more, faster. That's what you want to do: absorb as much as you can, as fast as you can, so you can move on.

In addition, the tedium of the study routine and workload, and the pressure of having to do well, is made worse by the fact that you'll be itching to get into the real world of Wall Street. You'll take occasional strolls down to the trading floor or sit in on some investment bank deal discussions and get really excited and really frustrated, knowing that you can't play with the pros yet. In fact, you won't be playing with them for quite some time, so keep that frustration in check.

GRADUATING TO ANALYST

As we've said, not everyone makes it through training. The underperformers who actually manage to slip through the door—the ones who look good on paper and sound good during the interviews but don't really amount to much when it comes to getting the hang of the basics—get jettisoned. But if you make it through, congratulations! You are graduating to the analyst program, where you'll join the more experienced hires that escaped training.

If you thought the hard stuff was over once you made it through training—the long hours, the lack of sleep, the studying, the heavy workload, the discomfort of feeling stateless, the frustration of not being able to join the real world—think again. In fact, the real torture starts once you're an analyst—so much torture, in fact, that you'll look back on your training days with some fondness.

A typical analyst program is based on rotating through several of the firm's divisions, spending a few months in each one and doing a whole host of jobs—some important, some menial, and some downright ridiculous. The idea is to give you some valuable, practical, hands-on experience to complement what you've just learned in the textbooks and case studies (though just how valuable and practical you'll probably wonder when you're standing in front of the photocopy machine at 10 P.M. on a Friday night, making thousands of copies of some document for an investment banker).

As an analyst you'll put in longer hours, and work even harder, than you did during training—going all day, all night, pulling a very heavy workload and running just to stay in place. You'll basically become one of Wall Street's pack mules. Worse, you'll be a pack mule that simply can't stumble—because if you do, you'll be shown the door. Everyone will be watching what you say and do, how you act and react, and how hard and enthusiastically you work. They'll do the same for all your peers, too, and the bottom tier, the folks who just don't put in enough effort, get culled. Unless you do a really solid job as an analyst, you won't get promoted to the next level, associate, meaning your Wall Street career is over. You can remain an associate for years and years, but analysts have an expiration date—it's strictly up or out—and that means it's the real make-or-break time for every new Wall Streeter (and make-or-break time that seems relentless, because it lasts for a few years).

SWALLOW YOUR PRIDE, HARD AND OFTEN

Swallowing your pride may be one of the hardest things for you to do as an analyst. If you think you're smarter than everyone else it will be very hard—especially when you're asked to do very menial tasks. But don't fight the system, just do as you're told. Remember, if you have trouble swallowing your pride, you'll have trouble getting through your analyst rotation and trouble making it on Wall Street. You have to learn your place and bide your time, and go through the same experiences that every other Wall Street veteran has gone through—you're not the first one doing this.

Of course, as an analyst you'll get to do some worthwhile things. You'll get to work on investment banking deal mechanics, price some financial instruments, help close the accounting books for quarter-end, trace operational flows to see where they break down—valuable jobs that give you hands-on experience in the ways of Wall Street and show you how it's all supposed to work. But you'll also do some menial, even stupid, things—including tasks you wouldn't have dreamed of doing when you were still in school or at one of your previous jobs. And you have to do them quickly, efficiently, and with a smile. Because your superiors, just like Orwell's Big Brother, are watching you—your performance, your attitude, your willingness.

What sorts of menial things? You name it: creating silly, multicolor Powerpoint presentations for bankers, photocopying thick prospectuses and legal documents, clipping news and magazine articles, making travel arrangements for client marketing trips (aka roadshows), booking hotel reception halls for client cocktail parties, and, yes, going down to Starbucks with the daily coffee orders. Oh, and if you have thoughts of working as a trader one day, you'd better get the orders right. Think about it: if you can't get the "one large Frappuccino, one medium skim Mochaccino, two grande half-caff lattes, three dopios, one single decaf Macchiatto, one tall Americano with room, two grande Sumatrans, two venti hot chocolates, and one small iced Chai" right, without pencil and paper, how on earth are you ever going to be able to buy 100 on-the-run long bonds at 99.5 dirty, buy 50 when-issued 5 years at 99.25, buy 250 off-the-run 10 years at par, sell 100 each in the belly at par 10, sell 200 20-year strips at 72.50, resell the 250 10 years at par 25, sell 100 10-year June bond futures at 99.75, sell 100 10-year September par 25 strike calls, and pay $100 million in swaps at 10 over the 10-year, all within three minutes, when it matters—that is, with real money at stake? No joke.

No doubt you'll think the menial tasks should be the domain and responsibility of secretaries and assistants, and you'll probably rebel a bit, because no one told you during the interview process that you'd be putting your college education and prior work experience to such poor use. Too bad, that's Wall Street. It's a unique mechanism for putting everyone on equal footing, to have them go through some humbling experiences and do the same awful grunt work, to pay dues before joining the club. Everyone has to do it, so swallow your pride, and do the best job you can. If you do it all well—ahead of schedule and with enthusiasm and a smile—you might get some payback when it comes time to rotate. If you do it all poorly or with a bad attitude, people will remember and relegate you to some outpost or lousy job—or just blow you out the door. (To help you along, think of the day when it'll be your turn to send an analyst up to the company library to photocopy 10 years' worth of financial statements on the 300 largest oil and gas companies operating in North America. Or to get customized coffee drinks for the entire 65-person oil and gas M&A team that you are managing. There is a kind of justice, you just have to wait your turn.)

FORGET ABOUT YOUR PERSONAL LIFE

As an analyst, a Wall Street pack mule, you have to forget about your personal life. Put all nonwork aspects of your life—relationships, interests, hobbies—on hold for a few years, because you will have neither the time nor the inclination to pursue anything that's not connected to the job.

If you're single, forget about any type of social contact. No dates, no movies, no fun weekends by the beach or in the mountains. Forget about the fact that you are in the Big City, with all those interesting and attractive men and women who are dying to meet you (and vice versa). Forget about the culture and the nightlife—the museums and theater, the concerts and ballet, the bars and restaurants. Forget about the fact that you actually have a few dollars of disposable income for the first time in your life (just a few, though, because you're probably paying an exorbitant amount for rent)—dollars that you are burning to spend, but just can't (think of it is a sort of cruel, forced-savings plan). If you're married, things aren't going to be much better. Your spouse will be thoroughly upset with you by the time this whole thing is over. Not only won't he or she see much of you, but on those rare occasions when you do meet you're likely to be in a zombielike state, able only to grunt affirmative or negative responses—probably not the reason you got married.

Also, forget about sleep. You are about to embark on an extended period of sleep deprivation, which is, again, a part of Wall Street's quirky hazing process. In a way it's kind of like college, where you would get up in the morning, go to a few classes, study, do your research projects or case studies, eat, and then progress from social event to social event, until some ungodly hour (maybe 4 A.M.), go home, have a two-hour nap, and start all over again. Only in this case you are replacing the recreational activities with huge volumes of work, and it's work of the very worst kind: deal-related, meaning time-sensitive. That means serious deadlines, probably under the ruthless, rude direction of an investment banker—someone you have to be nice to, since he/she will have a hand in your future at the firm. You just stay until the job is done. Period.

Wall Street doesn't really care about your personal life. There is work to be done, and you are going through the "trial by fire" stage, so you have to do all of the ugly but ultimately necessary work that needs to be done. Plan on being at work for 12, 14, 16, or even 18 hours a day, and to take work home with you for the weekends. Just put human existence on hold for a while.

GET THOSE COMPUTER SKILLS RAZOR SHARP

As you get into the swing of being an analyst you'll quickly learn that Wall Streeters love to give bosses and clients slick presentations with lots of important numbers, that they need to make lots of calculations, and that they have to manage and manipulate tons of data. Colorful presentations with graphs, spreadsheets with numbers, and databases chock-full of details are the lifeblood of modern finance, used to justify budgets, project the economics of deals and pitch all sorts of things to clients (in pretty colors and easy-to-digest bites).

So your computer skills need to be honed to razor sharpness. Bone up on all of those Microsoft goodies—Excel and Powerpoint and Access. Keep at them until you become a whiz (you'll know you're getting good when you start thinking about things in terms of keystrokes, cell formulas, color palettes, data axes, pivot tables, and bar chart options—it's a bit eerie). You'll use these tools constantly as an analyst, so the more you know, the quicker you can do the work, the sooner you can move on to the next project (or maybe even go home). And, if you get to be extremely proficient—able to do very complicated things on your computer very efficiently—then you'll have a vital and highly marketable skill that you should publicize when you rotate through different areas. When traders, salespeople, and bankers learn the kind of computing gymnastics you can do with spreadsheets, databases, and presentations, they will be like bees to honey. (And if you can get into supremely "techie" things like programming in Visual Basic or C++, you'll be in real demand. Play it up and leave them salivating. An analyst that knows bond math and C++ and can handle 20 Starbucks orders in his or her head is not to be taken lightly—real potential.)

MAKE LOTS OF CONTACTS DURING YOUR ANALYST ROTATION BECAUSE IT'S YOUR FUTURE

In the last chapter we said that you should take advantage of all your contacts to get in the door. The same is true once you are actually through the door. A typical analyst program calls for you to do a series of rotations through different business and control departments, so you can learn as much about the firm, and the industry, as possible. The rotations also help the firm find the most appropriate "permanent home" for you, a home where everyone benefits—you, the department and the firm.

In most firms, analysts are assigned to three to six rotations, each lasting from three to six months. Unfortunately, the training and human resource folks only map out your first and second rotations—the rest is up to you. That means you've got to be resourceful, finding your next home(s) on your own, as quickly as possible (remember that all your supercompetitive analyst colleagues are scouting out the same opportunities). Swallow your pride (again), make contacts in other areas, and "chat up" the bankers, the researchers, the treasury folks, the sales and trading groups— wherever you have an interest and think you can contribute. You've got to demonstrate your enthusiasm and capabilities to as many folks as you can, so that you increase your chances of landing in a good area when you graduate from the analyst program.

Unfortunately, it's usually pretty awkward and uncomfortable trying to line up your next gig. Experienced Wall Streeters can spot analysts on the rotation prowl from several hundred feet away—the look of nervousness, fear, inexperience—and often turn away in order to avoid getting hit up for a rotation request (so much for camaraderie and teamwork). Never mind—be aggressive and just keep pressing till you get some response. How? First of all, never schedule a formal meeting with any of these targets, as they'll just cancel on you at the last minute . . . time after time after time. Better to buttonhole them in the hallway and plead your case in 30 seconds or less. Then follow up by bursting into their office (or catching them at their desk on the trading floor) with Starbucks and doughnuts for the whole department. That often works. Then repeat this again, till you've covered the 20 or 30 departments on your short list. Be tenacious, because this is your future on Wall Street. If you don't press hard, you'll wind up getting dumped into an area that is decidedly not where you want to be—settlements, infrastructure, audit, or regulatory reporting. Then you might as well not be on Wall Street.

PATIENCE IS A VIRTUE AND A NECESSITY

Patience is an absolute necessity when you are an analyst. You've got to learn to bide your time. Even though you're probably bursting with energy, enthusiasm, and great ideas, you're not ready yet. Just concentrate, work hard (even at those awful little tasks) and be patient, or you'll go crazy. The hierarchy and rigidity and occasional stupidity of this stage of your Wall Street career will frustrate you, but just get over it. Before you know it, you'll be immersed in a very fluid world, where the rules change, the deals and markets move, the politics flare, and much of the structure that is so constraining just disappears. Till then, patience.

If you're patient and hardworking and you make it through your rotations successfully, you'll graduate. Again, not everyone makes it through the analyst program. Some get bounced, others decide they would rather go work in another industry, and some wash out and try again at some other firm.

But if you make it, congratulations! That means you've been promoted to associate and landed in one of the line or staff functions that you rotated through. You're no longer stateless or in professional limbo. You'll get your own business cards (with phone number and e-mail address) and start developing a closer bond with the firm (and you'll want to start wearing the company sweatshirt when you go to the gym for a workout). You've done it!

Or have you?

ASSOCIATES ARE GLORIFIED
SUPERANALYSTS WITH ACCOUNTABILITY

Just when you think it's over, it's not. As an associate you are in one of the most difficult spots in the Wall Street pecking order, caught between two worlds. Your bosses will expect you to do all the work of an analyst (e.g., all the spreadsheet stuff, all the presentation preparation, some of the photocopying, some of the travel and roadshow details) *and* start thinking and acting like a businessperson. Analysts are insulated from the commercial realities of the business (e.g., making client contacts, generating business, implementing controls), but associates are not. That means doing double duty. That means a few extra packs on the mule. That means even less personal life, less sleep and more tension, more stress.

And unfortunately, it's a process that can last for an indefinite amount of time. You'll be an associate for a period that can last several years. There is no hard-and-fast rule for the time it takes to get promoted from associate to assistant vice president (AVP, at which point you get to start dumping on other analysts and associates). It depends on the individual, the job they do, their boss(es), and the state of the market. Some associates get promoted after six months (deservedly so) and some after three years (deservedly so). If you can't get promoted after three years, you may find that Wall Street isn't your calling after all—and your boss may feel the same way. Sayonara. That may be the unkind truth after all the effort you have put in.

EARNING YOUR STRIPES

When you're an associate, you're finally in a position to earn your stripes— to prove your worth to yourself, your colleagues, your firm, and Wall Street. All the training and analyst work you've done has been in preparation for this because, as an associate, you can actually make a difference. As an associate you finally earn some legitimacy within the firm and get the power to make decisions. Even though you still rank very low on the totem pole, you're actually on the totem pole. Investment bankers, traders, risk managers, controllers, auditors, and others you come in contact with will recognize that you have the right to speak, give an opinion, or make a decision. And this means that, for the first time since landing on Wall Street, you'll actually be able to contribute to winning business or helping the firm with its controls or strategy. You'll be given some very important work to do—work that you'll be responsible for and that has a tangible end result. Which means you will know, very clearly, whether you are succeeding or failing.

When you're an analyst you're given a small piece of the puzzle to work on or take care of. As an associate, you're given the whole puzzle and the task of putting it all together (you'll still need some help, of course, but at least you've got all the pieces). So even though the work is hard (and you still have to do some of the unenviable analyst grunt work) the responsibility is rewarding—and that's what you really want as a professional. Now you've got the chance to prove that you can do it, that you have good ideas, that you can bring in business or solve a problem. You can finally start running with the big dogs on the trading floor, in investment banking or research. This is your first real opportunity to earn your Wall Street stripes, so go earn them.

START BECOMING INDISPENSABLE

The single most important thing you need to take away from your trainee, analyst, and associate days is the art of becoming indispensable. If you learn nothing else during that two- or three-year period, learn that. Wherever you are working, you've got to make it so that your department, team, and boss feel that they simply can't operate as effectively when you're not around. They must be made to feel like they can always turn to you for a good, thorough, and efficient job.

How do you do this? Anticipation and efficiency. You've got to learn to anticipate—to sense—what needs to be done before it actually becomes a request or requirement. Go the extra mile without being asked. And you need to get it done quickly and properly. Present your boss, as a fait accompli, projects and work accomplished through your own motivation and volition, and he or she will start to take notice. Do it efficiently and accurately and he or she will be even more impressed. Do it with enthusiasm and a good attitude, and you're going places. This all means hard work and thinking a few steps ahead—which you should be doing anyway if you want to succeed on Wall Street.

Becoming indispensable isn't intended as a political tactic or as a way of trying to show that you're the boss's "boy" or "girl." It is intended to show that you can, and do, care about doing a good job and about helping the firm move forward. Of course, if you keep it up, it'll have its benefits and rewards, mostly in the shape of promotions and bonuses. More important, though, your reputation will precede you, and you'll gain the respect of others higher up in the firm—and that can have long-term benefits in terms of visibility and mobility. And remember, this isn't just for analysts and associates. Even though you've got to learn it and apply it in the early stages of your Wall Street days, you should make it part of your "standard operating procedure" throughout your career, no matter your position, job, or function.

So as you've made it to associate, you've started to see a bit of Wall Street and how it works. Now let's look at the different jobs and personalities that are out there to see where you really fit in.

The Right Match: Finding Your Ideal Job

If you're new to Wall Street and have gone through the training program and the analyst rotation, you'll be joining the real world as an associate, in some part of the firm, when you finish. This means you will finally have a *real Wall Street job*. (If you're an "experienced" new hire, avoiding the training/analyst programs by filling a specific position that you're already qualified for [e.g., a CPA joining the accounting department, a lawyer joining the legal department, a risk manager joining the corporate risk department], you can skip ahead to the next chapter.)

But what job? Where are you actually going to work?

As we noted in chapter 3, this depends on the success you had during the analyst rotation cycle:

- Did you make the right contacts?
- Did you demonstrate enthusiasm for, and pledge undying allegiance to, various desks/business units/departments?
- Did you work like a pack mule, putting in lots of hours, pulling all-nighters and meeting all deadlines?
- Did you do your work with good cheer?

- Did you tell potential bosses how your experiences would benefit the group and how your good ideas and insight would help move things forward?
- Did you dazzle potential bosses with your technical skills?
- Did you socialize with would-be colleagues a bit, join them for Happy Hour or coffee, so that they could see how you act on a personal level, away from work?

If you did these things, you may get your pick of jobs. If you didn't, just accept what you get—remember that you can always transfer or rotate to some other area later on (if you do a good job, of course).

Wall Street jobs, not surprisingly, revolve around the five functions we talked about in chapter 1.

THE FIVE FUNCTIONS OF WALL STREET

Let's briefly review the five functions to set the stage:

- Function #1: Wall Street raises money for people, companies, and countries.
- Function #2: Wall Street buys and sells stocks and bonds and other things.
- Function #3: Wall Street tells companies and countries what to do with their money.
- Function #4: Wall Street tells people what to do with their money.
- Function #5: Functions #1, #2, #3, and #4 . . . all at once.

Function #1, raising money, is generally the responsibility of *investment banking.* Bankers spend lots of time on the road talking to people, companies, and countries, persuading them to borrow or sell bonds or stocks; when a bond or stock deal is ready to go, the bankers work with their colleagues from *trading* and *sales* to price it and sell it.

Function #2, buying and selling all kinds of assets, is the responsibility of *trading*, the group of people who make the two-way prices and protect themselves against any risk that might remain (this is what a dealer does) or just match up two different buy and sell orders (this is what an agent does), and *sales*, the members of which talk to retail and institutional clients and persuade them to sell or buy. These folks are also supported by employees in *research*, who analyze particular assets and markets and recommend things that should be bought or sold.

Function #3, telling companies and countries how to expand, acquire, contract, or turn themselves around, is also the domain of investment banking—again, bankers are constantly out trolling for new corporate finance, buyout, takeover, or restructuring opportunities.

Function #4, telling people what to do with their money, falls to the folks in *retail sales*. In addition to selling people things coming from Function #1, they also give financial advice regarding retirement plans, taxes, and insurance—so they really like to be known as financial advisors. Whatever.

Function #5, which involves getting everyone in the same room at the same time, is really difficult. But when it happens, it touches on each one of the groups above. Everyone has a part to play (and when it works, it's truly something to behold).

Surrounding all of these "glamorous" jobs are the slightly more mundane control, or staff, jobs. Though these seem a bit boring, they're absolutely vital in order to keep the juggernaut afloat—without control you can be sure that the ship will hit the first iceberg in its path and go down, end of story. So this is where control groups, like *accounting, financial control, risk management, audit, operations,* and *legal,* come in. These specialists make sure that the financial numbers are good, the risks are kept in check, the firm doesn't run into any legal problems, and that trades, deals, and transactions are settled properly. They're always working hard to keep the ship on a safe course.

So, with this landscape in mind, it's time for the next step.

FIGURE OUT WHAT YOU LIKE TO DO, AND THEN FIGURE OUT WHAT YOU'RE SUITED FOR

You can see that there are lots of different kinds of jobs on Wall Street—all with varying degrees of responsibility, pressure, and compensation—so you've got to find out where you fit. The first thing is figuring out what really interests you:

- Are you excited by calling on clients and working on deals late into the night?
- Do you like the energy of the trading floor, and do you get excited when you see trades being executed?
- Do you enjoy discovering hidden investment opportunities by analyzing the inner workings of companies and markets?
- Do you like to put together balance sheets and profit estimates and reconcile deals and trades?

This is the first step in the process. If you're totally new to Wall Street you want to try to work at something that interests you. You'll be more motivated and energized, and you'll do a better job. And if you're already an experienced professional (about to make a switch to The Street because you can't stand your current job), then you know how important it is, when you're working 12 or 14 hours a day, to be doing something you really like.

But, wait, there's a second step. Once you know what interests you, you've got to determine what you're really suited for. Sometimes these are one and the same, sometimes they aren't. For example, you may be very interested in being a trader, but your personality suggests you're better suited for accounting. Even though you might be able to stretch and become a trader, you're probably not going to do well at it or even enjoy it—trading and accounting are two different worlds populated by two different personalities.

To help you put some of this in perspective, check your personality and characteristics against this "personality road map":

If you are . . .	*Then you likely are suitable for . . .*
Rigid, risk-averse, detail-oriented, don't like to go too fast, and don't want to live too close to the edge of the cliff	Accounting, financial control, risk management, audit, operations, legal
Creative and risk-loving, a free spirit who likes to go hard 24/7 and stand right on the edge of the cliff	Investment banking, trading, institutional sales, retail sales
Aggressive, with good memory and multi-tasking skills, but short attention span	Trading
Aggressive, arrogant, slick, well-spoken, and very good in social situations	Investment banking
Aggressive, arrogant, slick, and very good in social situations, but not the sharpest knife in the drawer	Institutional sales
Aggressive, thick-skinned, fast-talker, able to handle rejection, but not the sharpest knife in the drawer	Retail sales
Smart, able to serve many masters, in love with the limelight, and willing to put it all on the line	Research

Once you've figured out what you enjoy and where you fit personality-wise—let's hope they don't diverge too much—you can point yourself in the right direction. By the time you're finishing up your analyst rotations you'll be ready to commit to a particular group.

But there are other Wall Street "career truisms" that you should be aware of—they can help tip the balance in one direction or another.

CORPORATE STAFFERS: THE BUREAUCRATIC POLICE

There is a great divide on Wall Street between businesspeople (aka producers) and corporate staff people (aka controllers, police)—those responsible for leading the charge on the five functions and those responsible for making sure things don't blow up. There is a definite "us versus them" mentality, where "we" try to maximize the firm's earnings and "they" try to stop business deals that are too risky or dangerous.

In general, producers have little tolerance for police. They like to drive down the highway at 125 mph and hate getting pulled over for a speeding violation. That takes all the fun out of the job. The cops, of course, view their enforcement actions as wise safety measures, as a way of protecting those who might injure themselves or others (a bit like taking sharp scissors away from kids). And that's not a bad thing, because no one really wants to get hurt. The bottom line, though, is that bankers, traders, and salespeople want the freedom to act—to do business, generate revenues for the firm, and, of course, maximize the bonus pool. Anything or anyone who stands in their way is cutting the number of dollars in the year-end pay packet.

This attitude and perspective are, of course, a bit naïve. Sure, control staff can be stiff and overly bureaucratic at times. And they aren't the most exciting folks on earth (they talk about debits, credits, and reserves instead of the point spread on Sunday's football game). But, the truth is that these folks regularly save overexuberant and sloppy traders, salespeople, and bankers from walking off the edge of the cliff. They are the necessary counterbalance to all of the creativity—all of the "pushing the edge of the envelope"—that lives on Wall Street. Absent these police, Wall Street would be a very ugly place.

So don't dismiss them, and don't discount working in a control area when you're trying to figure out the job scene. (And bear in mind this little-known secret: control folks can get paid as much as producers . . . and they have much greater job security when times are bad. More on this later.) However, if you are firmly of the "us" mentality, you should focus your efforts on a producing job—investment banking, trading, or sales.

PRODUCERS: THE SLIPPERY AND EGOCENTRIC

Staff professionals don't trust producers. They are wary of their intentions and find them slippery. They think they're all two-faced, able to speak only with forked tongues. And they know that they're driven primarily by ego. Their views tend to be shaped by real experience: staffers are constantly chasing after producers, like a mother goose after her goslings—keeping them in line, telling them what to do, reminding them for the umpteenth time what not to do and chastising them when they've gone and done it again. Staff pros spend a lot of time baby-sitting these folks and cleaning up their messes. Little wonder they don't trust them or like them. Staffers don't understand why mature, producing professionals can't be more diligent about following the rules, doing things properly, and supporting the firm in its efforts to operate in a controlled way. When everyone plays by the rules, everyone benefits, right?

Still, producers aren't all that bad. Not all of them are 100 percent ego-driven or tough to deal with, and many actually have good intentions—they just need a little work on their manners and a bit more discipline when it comes to postdeal details (aka "the boring stuff that has to get done once the deal-induced adrenaline rush wears off"). Producers have lots of things on their minds, so attention to the little things sometimes slips. They are just creative spirits trying to express themselves, but in a financial way rather than with a canvas or musical instrument. They don't mean any harm. And in the midst of their frustrations and venting, staffers still have to remember that Wall Street exists because producers produce. That's the bottom line. Bankers, traders, and salespeople generate the cash that pays for the overhead, holiday parties and year-end bonuses, so they deserve a little slack (but not so much that they hang themselves, the department, or the whole firm).

So if you want to bring money in the door, be creative, and drive hard and fast, you should think about being a producer. But if you are more in synch with the "them" personality, consider a job in finance, operations, treasury, or risk management—remember, the dollars are good, and the job security is better.

INVESTMENT BANKERS AS PRIMA DONNAS, TRADERS AS ORDER TAKERS

Lest you think that the us-versus-them attitude is limited to producers and staffers, you should be made aware that some of the biggest personality splits actually occur within the businesses. For instance, there is no love lost between traders and investment bankers.

Traders view investment bankers as prima donnas—as arrogant, temperamental, high-strung globetrotters in tailored $4,000 suits and eye-popping Hermes ties and scarves; as people who never take the subway to work (taxi, car service, or limo only, please); as people who absolutely must vacation at all the right Caribbean and Rocky Mountain resorts; as people who just have to have a summer home in the Hamptons to be part of the "in" crowd; as people who may be good at talking and selling to CEOs, but are disconnected from the organic side of Wall Street (the price-making, the frenzied buying and selling, the market gyrations, the large losses and [we hope!] larger profits). Any trader will tell you that banking is a slow, boring, high-gloss sales function. Deals are slow to build, require mountains of legal documentation and take forever to conclude (generally over pricey dinners in posh restaurants). That's not the "real" Wall Street, that's just dull. Even though the deals the bankers string together—mergers, acquisitions, buyouts, takeover defenses, capital restructurings, tax plays—can yield juicy fees, traders will always tell you that banking is a soft life and carries none of the real pressure of trading.

Bankers, for their part, will tell you that traders just don't get it: banking is about cultivating senior relationships in order to win high-quality, high-margin repeat business for the firm. It requires polish, culture, intelligence, diplomacy, and quiet cajoling at opportune moments (such as a nice lunch just before the CEO is to decide which firm should get the three-year acquisition and financing program). And any banker will tell you that traders don't have a clue about real pressure—about winning megadeals so that the firm can eat well for months or years. What happens if you miss? How many megadeals come around each year? That's pressure—that's Wall Street.

Bankers view traders as just so many fast-food order clerks. What's the difference between selling a fund manager 10,000 GM bonds (at 99 each) and a hungry teenager three double cheeseburgers (at 99 cents each)? None, as far as the banker is concerned. Traders (after completing the string of colorful expletives that is second nature to them) will tell you that trading is all about knowing how and where to buy the bonds for 98.5 and knowing that they should be sold for 99 (not 98.75 or 99.25). That's a skill born of many years in the trenches—years of losses and profits, of going home with large risk positions and not sleeping through the night, of not being able to hedge properly, of having clients walk away on trades (aka "DK")—in short, all of the high-pressure situations that bankers simply wouldn't even begin to understand. Bankers just think traders are there to service their needs. After all, bankers generate all the new issue and financing deals that create the securities that traders trade. So without bankers, there wouldn't be any supply of securities, and traders would be unemployed. Right?

The reasons for these polar views are cultural, social, and educational. Lots of traders come from the rough-and-tumble world of lower-middle-class neighborhoods, public schools, junior colleges, and state universities. That breeds the aggressive, in-your-face attitude that is almost a prerequisite for trading. Lots of investment bankers come from the well-to-do suburbs, private prep schools, and Ivy League universities. That breeds the refinement and diplomacy that is necessary when courting top management at client firms. The first time many of these folks actually meet and interact is during the training and analyst programs. The coarse and rough future traders are befuddled by the WASPy, preppy future bankers, and vice versa. Bridging that divide is almost impossible, and usually happens only for short bursts of time (30 minutes to 24 hours)—when the bankers need tight pricing from the traders on new-issue deals and the traders want to get securities out the door. Everyone is friendly and cooperative for a while and gets the deal done. Then it's back to the reality of separate worlds. So as you are thinking about where you belong, think about the differences between these two producers. Even though they are on the same side of the fence, they are very, very different animals.

TRADERS ARE NOT CREATED EQUAL

It would be nice to say that all traders view themselves in the same light—as a cohesive group that can stand up against bankers and salespeople, a brotherhood/sisterhood, a union, strength in numbers. But they can't. Sure, traders all work on the same floor. Many come from the same background (even neighborhood) and often have the same kind of drive, mentality, and personality. But even within the rough-and-tumble world of trading there are some real differences. And among those are differences that breed conflict, jealousies, and more than a little infighting.

On the two extremes of the trading spectrum we find "brute-force" traders and "intellectual" traders (almost an oxymoron as far as bankers are concerned); sandwiched in between are the "smart brute-force" traders.

Brute-force traders are the ones who buy simple things cheap and sell them rich—things like stocks, currencies, or Treasury bonds. A buy price and a sell price, that's all they need to know, and they get to keep whatever's left in the middle. Sure, they'll tell you that it's much, much more complicated than that—that they need to know about what the big institutional buyers are doing, whether the short sellers are active, the state of the new-issue pipeline, interest rate parity and cross-rates, macroeconomic policy, retail sales, how to manage the remaining risk in their book, and how long it'll take to get rid of something that they don't like. That's all true, but it still isn't that complicated. Brute-force trading tends to be very low-profit, high-volume stuff, so real money is made based on activity—the more volume, the better the day. Brute-force traders often like to boast how much flow they're trading and how many tickets they're writing. It's a mark of their success.

At the other end of the trading spectrum are the traders who know lots of math and can put together, or take apart, very complicated deals, structures, and financial relationships in order to make money, often lots of money. These are folks who trade derivatives (buying and selling special contracts that are based on the assets that brute-force traders deal in) or run "arbitrage" books (buying and selling things based on price discrepancies that they think will eventually make them money). Lots of them have PhDs in math or physics and do calculus for fun during their coffee breaks. Much of their money is made on large, high-margin deals, so they don't have to do quite as much daily ticket writing as their brute-force colleagues (they view all that ticket writing as real order taking, so maybe the investment bankers are right?). Their mark of success comes when they can make their monthly budget on a single deal.

And in between the two are the smart brute-force traders who buy and sell things that are more complicated than stocks or currencies, but not as complicated as derivatives. Things like corporate bonds (the IOUs we talked about in chapter 1) and convertible bonds (IOUs that can be changed into stock) and mortgage-backed securities (IOUs secured by home mortgages). These require a little more intellectual capacity than stocks or currencies, but are still pretty high-volume/low- margin deals.

There's no love lost between any of these groups. Brute-force traders think the intellectual traders are snobby because they know lots of math (and are a bit jealous of the amount of money they can make on a single deal). Intellectual traders think their brute-force colleagues are simpletons (though they admire the daily volume they get to trade), and the smart brute-force traders think they are surrounded by snobs and simpletons. In the end, they all need each other. The intellectual traders need to trade the flow of the brute-force traders, the brute-force traders need to hedge their risk with the intellectual traders, and they all need each other to stand up against bankers and salespeople. So if you think you've got the trading personality in your blood, see which of these groups you fit into.

BANKERS ARE NOT CREATED EQUAL

Just as the trading floor is a mix of pedigree and mongrel, mathematical elegance and down-and-dirty market aggression, so too the banking world. Investment banking in a big firm is a mélange of generalists and specialists, the big-picture folks and the technical experts, the relationship types and the mechanics. They don't care much for each other, but, like their trading brethren, they need each other, so they try and tolerate each other's differences.

Bankers come in a few different flavors: relationship managers, corporate finance generalists, and industry/deal specialists. The relationship bankers are the big-big-big-picture folks who have very contact-rich Rolodexes/Palm Pilots and know how to charm and impress their clients. They can wax eloquent for hours about a lot of general business and banking topics, but can't talk for more than a minute about the nuts and bolts of a complicated banking product or deal. They play lots of golf with chairmen and CEOs, CFOs and finance ministers, talking high-level strategy about what the client needs to do to get ahead. This is all very important to win business—relationship managers exist to bag the deal mandates.

But, since the "investment banking devil" is certainly in the details, they need to fall back on their specialist colleagues—the ones who actually know how to put deals together and book the revenues. Corporate finance generalists can do lots of things, usually quite well. They are very capable jacks-of-all-trade (though never *primus inter pares*). Think of them as utility players on a football team: they can play fullback or tight end, and can even go on defense and play middle linebacker. They don't have the connections or savoir faire of their relationship management colleagues, but they are good in front of clients and actually know how to put basic "vanilla" deals together—acquisitions, spin-offs, buyouts, regular new issues—so they're actually smarter than relationship managers.

However, even they don't have all the answers. So when things get really specialized and complex—maybe a client wants to move on a hostile takeover or leveraged buyout, a special-purpose tax-dodge vehicle, a very complicated cross-border securities issue, or a corporate reorganization in a highly regulated industry—they call on the specialist bankers: the folks who really have all the answers. Specialist bankers are deal and product mechanics who know *everything* about their chosen field: the intricacies of accounting rules, the legal and regulatory barriers affecting specific industries, the legal construction of takeover defenses, ways to boost cash flows but lower earnings to reduce taxes, the best exit strategies for management buyouts. They know how and where to look for loopholes (legal ones, of course) so that the deal works. But since specialists know so much, they can be quite geeky—meaning they really aren't meant to interact with clients. (In fact, an unwritten banking rule prohibits a specialist from seeing a client without a relationship manager along as chaperone. If it's absolutely necessary to put specialist bankers in front of clients to explain what's going to happen on a deal, they need to be accompanied—and preferably coached in advance—by relationship managers.)

The interactions between relationship managers, corporate finance generalists, and specialists are tense but symbiotic. In the end, they still need to stand up against the traders. So if you want in on the investment banking action, figure out which group suits you best. They're very, very different.

THE MERCURIAL RESEARCH ANALYST: TOUT, HERO, GOAT

Researchers are intelligent folks who can look at companies, sectors, or entire markets, do some analysis, and then tell investors and clients what to buy or sell. They know a lot about accounting, so they can rip apart financial statements and figure out whether a company is making it or not, and they know a lot about the markets, so they can tell whether investors need to be buying or selling. They're plugged into their industries so they can tap into the gossip that happens away from financial statements. Good analysts can pick up the phone and talk to senior folks at companies they cover to try and figure out what's really happening (of course, that often puts them in contact with inside information, which they are supposed to treat with kid gloves so as not to run afoul of securities trading violations). Researchers basically live and breathe things like stock prices, price/earnings ratios, earnings per share, and credit spreads; what they really care about is whether something is cheap or rich so they can come up with a recommendation on what to do.

Every Wall Street research analyst tastes victory and defeat during his or her career—one day the hero, the next day the goat. It comes with the territory, because analysts make very public proclamations on what people should do with their investment dollars: buy, sell, or hold. Or, more precisely, multiple variations on those three choices, like strong buy, medium sell, overweight hold, underweight neutral, lukewarm buy with a negative bias (actually, analysts have a predilection for "buys"—hence their status as touts. Rarely does an analyst give out a "sell" recommendation). Their recommendations are public proclamations with a capital P in public. Analysts blanket the investor base with tens of thousands of printed research reports, appear on the CNBC and CNN, give interviews in the *Wall Street Journal, Financial Times, Forbes,* and *Fortune.* In short, they expose their recommendations to complete scrutiny. So if they're right, they're heroes, and if they're wrong, they're goats. Heroes can enjoy stardom for a while (though only a while, as everyone eventually gets it wrong); goats are soon forgotten and descend into relative obscurity.

As you're mulling over the hero/goat trade-off, you should note that researchers have a little extra baggage because of their multiple and sometimes conflicting allegiances. They can serve several masters at any one time, so it's not always clear for whom they really work:

- Do they work for the client, by giving unbiased opinions? They are, after all, supposed to make recommendations that help clients earn as much as they can on their investments.
- Do they work for investment bankers, by giving good recommendations on a client's securities so that the bankers can win more business? A firm isn't going to win much acquisition or financing business if its analyst is telling all the investing clients that the company is lousy and they should dump the stock.
- Do they work for someone else, like the trading department—giving some thoughts on what to buy or sell (based only on public information, and only after clients have been told . . . no inside dealing or front running. Right.)?

Although most firms have what's known as a "Chinese wall" separating the activities of research from investment banking and trading, it's not much of a wall. In fact, the wall usually has some gaping holes—more than a few analysts have been seen in the company of bankers, pitching hard for new business by giving out "buy" recommendations (basically, getting paid for helping bring in new investment banking deals instead of giving clients truly good, helpful, and unbiased advice). To wit, analysts who are true to their discipline (the anti-touts who do good, independent work and call the dogs dogs) don't have much job security—though that may change with the Janus-like role of the research analyst becoming clearer. These days you're apt to find research analysts over in insulated, independent units rather than cavorting around the world with investment bankers, so they can actually do the work they are supposed to (without aggressive bankers breathing down their necks and demanding good recommendations on their clients). That'll probably lead to better research in the long run, but who knows—it'll take some time to restore credibility—so you may want to steer clear for a few years, until these folks prove themselves once again.

INSTITUTIONAL SALESPERSON OR CAR DEALER?

Institutional salespeople sell stocks, bonds, and currencies to professional investors like Fortune 500 companies, pension funds, insurance companies, and investment managers. They also sell them those derivatives we mentioned above, and some of them are kind of toxic—things like US Dollar Libor leveraged inverse power floaters, quantoed into Japanese yen, with an outside barrier knocking out on the S&P 500 (don't even ask . . . just remember that everything has a buy price and sell price). And they do things on a large scale: millions, even hundreds of millions, of dollars per trade.

As a result, they think they are very, very important. They are very aggressive because they always seem to have a large trade hanging in the balance. They demand all attention and focus until the trade is done, and when it's done they go off happily, counting the sales credits they just earned (sales credits are used as part of the year-end bonus tally). Since they do big trades, they get lots of sales credits, meaning large bonuses (in contrast to their retail brethren, who do small trades and get small sales credits and small bonuses). Sales credits are everything to the institutional salesperson.

Institutional salespeople aren't necessarily the brightest bunch on the trading floor and sometimes don't really understand what they are selling—especially if it's something kind of complex (like that ugly thing we just mentioned). More than a few clients have been "blown up" (i.e., lost lots of money) over the years because salespeople didn't really understand what they were selling and clients didn't understand what they were buying. All they know is that the client isn't going to pay more than 99 for the $100 million trade, so if the trader quotes 99.25, you can bet all hell is going to break loose (sometimes institutional salespeople think they work for the client rather than the firm).

Though salespeople walk around the floor with a veneer of importance (even sophistication), most folks in the firm view them in a different light—as if they were car dealers. In fact, there are striking similarities: both sell important, expensive things, and both try to sell as much as they can so they can get more sales credits (and get bigger bonuses). These folks are still very important to Wall Street, because someone has to flog the securities that the bankers have arranged and the traders trade. It's just that what they do isn't very different than what car dealers do. Just compare the roles of institutional salesperson and car dealer: the process starts with a bit of sales talk over lunch in the company dining room (on the car lot) and then moves to some daily phone calls to review the "red hot" bonds in the computer (Mercedes on the lot). Then there is a bit of haggling on price, "Okay . . . but my final price is 99" ("Okay . . . but my final price is $99,000"), and the bond trade is done (Mercedes is sold). Later on, if the client wants to get rid of the bonds (car), the salesperson is ready to buy them back at an appropriate discount (trade-in value). And the salesperson is always ready to sell the client his or her next bonds (Mercedes).

If you've got some leanings in this direction, and you like cars, it might be the place for you.

RETAIL SALESPERSON OR TELEMARKETER?

Retail salespeople, the ones who sell stocks and bonds to Mom and Dad, are like those dreaded telemarketers who call at dinner to try to sell you magazine subscriptions or long-distance calling plans.

On Wall Street they are known, collectively and harshly, as the "great unwashed" (curiously enough the term seems to have stuck). These are the legions of cold-calling brokers who try to sell odd lots (small amounts of securities) by phoning unsuspecting people at home, reading off of manuscripts and making recommendations prepared by the research analysts. Their modus operandi is just like the telemarketer trying to sell you a subscription to *Sports Illustrated* or *Vogue*. You know the pitch: "You should buy this security [magazine] because it's good value for your money. It's priced to move and it'll bring you lots of enjoyment, and if you act now, I can throw in a commission-free trade [extra one-month subscription]. But you must act today."

Enough said. But Wall Street needs these folks because they need to connect to Main Street. Firms that can pump securities to the common folk have tremendous distribution power, which helps investment bankers win new deals. Think about it. If the banker can tell the CEO of the company planning to issue securities that it can blanket the entire country with shares or bonds, isn't that attractive? And, in fairness, really good retail salespeople are broadening their horizons by offering other services to clients they have cultivated (e.g., tax, retirement, wealth planning). But it all starts with those awful cold calls.

So if you are more comfortable being part of Wall Street through your local town or city, and you can take rejection well (all those irate Moms and

Dads slamming down the phones so they can get back to their dinners), this may be your job.

SINGLES AND DOUBLES, OR HOME RUNS?

We've talked a bit about the money angle in chapter 1. You are on Wall Street, or heading there, because the financial rewards can be very attractive. We'll talk about money again in chapter 10, but for now let's consider a few things related to money and the right job. It's actually very simple. If you want to maximize your earnings potential, you want to be some kind of producer. Producers generate revenues, and revenues translate directly into bonuses. Staffers, as we'll see later on, can get paid well, too, but generally not to the same degree. Producers can hit home runs—single-year paychecks of seven figures, occasionally eight figures—while staffers generally hit singles and doubles (though an excellent senior staffer can hit the long ball, too).

The downside of being a producer is, of course, a strikeout —a bad year. If you can't produce because the markets are bad or the clients aren't doing anything (or you're losing business to the competition) then you won't get paid as much. You'll be swinging for the home run with all your might, but miss. If you strike out too many times, you'll actually get booted off the team—and that doesn't tend to happen as much if you're swinging for singles or doubles. So, we're back to the cliff dweller scenario we mentioned in chapter 2. If you want to live on the edge of the cliff and get paid more, be prepared for the long drop down when or if you lose your job.

So as you think about your ideal job, think about the money angle, what it means to you, how focused you are on the number of zeros on your paycheck and how sensitive you are to changes in that paycheck from year to year—and how worried you are about possibly losing your job. If you want to have a go at hitting the ball out of the park—maximizing your earnings but taking more risk in the process, then you want to be an investment banker, a trader, a researcher, or a salesperson. If you prefer to play conservatively—living without those yearly "paycheck swings" and sleeping comfortably away from the edge of the cliff—you want to be an accountant, an auditor, a risk manager, or a lawyer.

Now that you know a bit about the jobs, how about habits and routines? Let's see what you need to know to get into the rhythm of Wall Street.

Good Behavior:
Habits to Help You Along

You've been through training, you've completed your analyst rotations, and you've found a solid job on the trading floor, in investment banking, or in one of the control functions. You're doing well as an associate, and maybe you've even made it to assistant vice president. Or perhaps you've joined the firm from graduate school or some other job, settled in, and hit your stride.

Either way, you're starting to develop a Wall Street mind-set now, and you probably understand a bit more about how the game is played. And even though you haven't mastered office politics, you are definitely starting to feel at home.

Establishing good habits can help make you feel even more comfortable, because they let you cope with the rigors and pressures of daily life on Wall Street. They put you "in the know," help you prioritize and work efficiently, and help you get things done—all vital to success on The Street. Before long you'll come up with your own working style—based on your personality and job function—so that you can handle the daily tasks and deadlines as if they were second nature. In the meantime, though, some helpful habits are worth developing.

FIGURE OUT WHAT'S GOING ON

You can't start your day without knowing what's happening—in the firm, in the markets, in the economy, and with the competition. That's because Wall Street's business is based on information. The core of its existence is based on knowing who's buying, who's selling, who's going under, what country is in trouble, what country needs money, where the economy is heading, how retail sales are faring, what the consumer is doing, how high credit card debt is, how slow housing starts are, where the dollar/yen rate is going, which Japanese bank is cracking, what the folks down the block are doing, who won the big M&A deal, who got stuck with the bad position, where the big bond deal cleared the market, and on and on. The firms that know these things win business because they can anticipate what is likely to happen and what needs to get done.

Because you are part of Wall Street, you need to know what's going on. Regardless of your job, you've got to be plugged into this information flow—you can't live in an information vacuum. Information will make your job easier; it'll make you a bit wiser (you'll seem to know what's really happening); and you'll probably be more interesting at social events (e.g., "Well, as you know, Brazil is going through some tough economic times, but with the IMF package, some structural import-based reforms, and some new dollar issuance this year—at 900 over 10 year Treasuries—I think the country will pull through and avoid an external debt renegotiation." Wow, they'll be falling at your feet).

So, your daily Wall Street routine should start with as much information as you can absorb in 30 or 60 minutes from newspapers, TV, or the Internet. Though there's lots of garbage, fluff, and irrelevant stuff in the media, you'll soon get in the habit of honing in on what's really important. When you uncover something relevant, dig deeper and figure out how it ties in to what you do and what the firm does. You'll be surprised how useful this becomes in your daily life.

PLUGGING THE INTERNAL INFORMATION GAP

One thing you'll learn very quickly if you're working in a firm with any sort of scope or scale is that internal information gaps are the rule, rather than the exception. The firm has "black holes" through which important data, information, and knowledge enter but never exit. That's not because there is something malevolent or malicious going on. It's because most firms have expanded their information technology piecemeal, over very long periods of time, and that means the systems used to run daily business just can't talk to each other. So important gaps appear, and the only way you can get these patched up is the old-fashioned way, by hand.

If your job requires you to know specific things about the markets, clients, and the firm's finances or its risks, you'll have to create your own information flow. Tap into the electronic sources that you have total faith in, ignore the ones that you know have lots of garbage, and pull out manual ones to fill in the holes. It's a bit antiquated in this day and age, but business has moved so rapidly that it has pretty much outstripped Wall Street's ability to keep pace. Replacing all of a firm's technology in one go, so that everything talks to everything else, is just too expensive and disruptive, so it's just not going to happen (hence the piecemeal approach).

It's very important for you to identify information gaps early on, because if you start operating with a key piece of the picture missing, it'll just be a question of time before some important details are missing from your decisions. You'll make the wrong call one day because you don't have something crucial, and all hell will break loose. So figure out what you need to know, where you can get it, where you can't get it, how you can still get at it, and how you can put it all together. Plug the holes, and you'll be that much smarter.

MULTITASKING IS EVERYTHING

On Wall Street you've got to be able to handle two, three, five, or ten things at a time. You have to be able to work on multiple calls, deals, trades, projects, reports, and presentations simultaneously, because that's the nature of the beast. Business deals drive Wall Street, and they never stop. And you have to do them all well, *and on time*. There is no such thing as sequential tasking on Wall Street—it's just too hectic for you to be able to take on one deal or project, see it through to completion, start on the next one and see that one through, and so forth.

Wall Street is impatient, so part of your daily routine starts with figuring out what absolutely, positively needs to get done during the day, making sure that it gets done, and then absorbing new calls, requests, queries, jobs, and tasks as they appear during the course of the morning, afternoon, and evening. You'll find that you soon develop a "tactical battle plan" approach and that much of your life revolves around dealing with very short-term pressures, often at the expense of long-term, strategic issues, which invariably get pushed to the back burner (try not to forget about them as you cope with the daily "firefighting").

If you want to see multitasking in its ultimate form, just watch a few of the firm's traders on the floor for a while: they know how to do it to perfection. Here you'll see a trader pick up one phone and buy some bonds, pick up a second phone and cradle it under his chin, punch up some numbers on the computer screen, sell some bonds, hang up the first line and pick up another call, buy some different bonds at a different price, put the call on mute and shout out an order to another trader to hedge the risk in the trading book, look up at the administrative assistant and mouth out a lunch order, scrawl details of the three trades just executed on a blotter, pick up a calculator and figure out how much he has just made, sip some coffee, pick up another call, put it on mute, scream some prices into the "hoot and holler" intercom to the sales desk, look up at the large TV monitors dotting the floor to see what CNBC is saying about oil prices (and what Maria Bartiromo is wearing), pick up another call and sell some more bonds, wave across the floor to his golf buddy on the convertible bond desk, pick up another line and buy some more bonds, and so on, all day long, without losing focus and without losing money. Every day. The same "multitasking ballet" happens in other parts of the firm, especially as deals come close to conclusion or financial results need to get reported. That's the way the place gets work done.

So in order to survive the daily flow of Wall Street, you've got to multitask. And in order to multitask, you've got to be extremely organized and extremely efficient. If you aren't organized and efficient, get some help, quickly.

NO PROCRASTINATING

With rare exception—mostly around the end of the year or when the markets are in the doldrums—Wall Street is always humming. Walk into any Wall Street firm, visit any trading floor, banking department, or control area, and you'll always see and hear some kind of activity. And it's real activity—not the fake sort that some employees pull to impress their bosses (or that entire companies pull to impress clients, regulators, and other distinguished visitors). That's because everyone is busy multitasking. Everyone is trying to meet deadlines that coincide with the daily, weekly, monthly, and quarterly deals and cycles.

When you're part of this environment, you quickly get in the habit of not procrastinating: never doing in 30 minutes what you can do in 10 minutes, never putting off till tomorrow what you can easily do today. Just when you think you've caught up on things and should take a bit of a breather, you'll find something else popping up or you'll have a good idea that will lead you to do something else. There is very little downtime. Even lunches and coffee breaks happen at desks, in offices, and in conference rooms, because there is literally no time to goof off if you want to stay on top of things.

In no time you'll find that you operate at a high level of energy and efficiency throughout the day (aided, of course, by your Starbucks fixes) and that procrastinating for even a little while feels alien and uncomfortable. If you aren't doing something useful and productive, you'll feel a bit guilty and go find something useful and productive to do.

BE PUNCTUAL EVEN IF
THE INVESTMENT BANKERS AREN'T

Since procrastination just doesn't work on Wall Street, you learn pretty quickly that almost everyone on The Street cherishes punctuality. If you can be punctual you'll find you've got time to do what needs to get done. If you can't, you'll forever be scrambling to catch up, and you'll probably irritate lots of folks. With Wall Street's relentless pace, there is nothing more frustrating than sitting around in a conference room with 20 other people—controllers, auditors, producers—waiting for the "main person" (the one who really needs to be there) to show up. This is idle time, and on Wall Street idle time means lost opportunities and lost revenues. (It's amazing how many really smart people, responsible for millions and millions of the firm's dollars, can't look at a watch or clock and realize that they need to be at a meeting.)

The exception to the "punctuality rule" is investment banking. As we said in the last chapter investment bankers are prima donnas—and since prima donnas like to make big entrances, they are, by nature and habit, always late. In fact, one of the unwritten job requirements for investment bankers is to be 15 to 30 minutes late for every internal meeting (not client meetings, of course—never keep the client waiting). That's because they are very important people and are *always* working on big, sensitive deals that will generate millions of dollars in fees for the firm. And they want you to know that. There is a way around this, of course, and that's for the meeting's leader (pray not an investment banker) to schedule a meeting for 12:30 and tell the investment banker it starts at noon. Everyone should arrive at about the same time. For all their smarts, bankers seem not to have caught on to this technique—it helps everyone remain punctual and get down to business.

UNPRODUCTIVE MEETINGS
CAN BE PRODUCTIVE—JUST PLAN AHEAD

The corporate world generally, and Wall Street specifically, likes to meet. For everything. That may be because it's a social mechanism, or a way for folks to hand out unwanted tasks or spread responsibility, or a break in the daily routine. Whatever the reason, Wall Street firms have lots of meetings, and many of them are unfocused and unproductive (sometimes even counterproductive, meaning another meeting has to be called to undo the results of the previous meeting).

After waiting for the latecomers to actually show up, meetings can meander into side issues and irrelevant conversations and, after a vain attempt by someone to get them back on track, end without conclusion or resolution. Take heart. If you plan ahead, you can use the time to your advantage by simply bringing along other work that needs to get done. The one-hour "pointless meeting" can actually become a one-hour "quiet period" where you get real work done. You just have to learn to tune out the side conversations, look up every so often and nod, maybe interject some comment. And try to be semidiscreet (e.g., don't bring your Blackberry to send e-mails)—you don't want everyone to get irritated by the fact that you are being productive while they aren't.

WHOM CAN YOU TRUST?

Wall Street is competitive: each person is looking out for his or her own interests. Since everyone wants to get ahead, they're not going to play nice. Even though corporate principles and ethics espouse things like "integrity" and "respect," you shouldn't be naïve—this is Wall Street, a combat zone where a colleague won't hesitate to let you take the bullet if it means getting ahead. So watch your back.

We'll talk a bit more about corporate politics in chapter 8, but for now let's talk about trust and how it can help you in your daily working life. If you're going to be effective and do a good job, you've got to figure out whom you can trust and whom you can't. In any stressful, high-pressure job you've got to unload. You need an outlet, someone you can talk to and confide in—someone with whom you can share your business ideas and concerns, or the things that worry, excite, and scare you—all without fear of something being used against you. If you can't share the load, you'll bottle it up and wind up doing things that are generally unhealthy.

It takes time to figure out whom to really trust. You've got to get to know your colleagues and your bosses, folks in other departments that you come in contact with, the firm's reporting lines and divisional politics. None of this is easy in a large firm, and it's all made a bit more difficult by the constant rotation that sweeps through most places. People come and go, folks get hired, fired, promoted, and reassigned, so the cast of characters is always changing. But it's worth the effort. If you can identify a handful of people you can really trust and develop a bond with them, then you create an essential outlet, a sounding board, a release mechanism. That can help you cope with the daily pressures of Wall Street. It can help you come up with good ideas, or it can provide some healthy, temporary distraction from the rigors of work. Just be careful when you're trying to figure out whom you should take into your confidence, and err on the side of not saying much till you're really sure. Otherwise the best of the firm's con men and con women will have you confessing and divulging everything, and you'll wind up hearing about it from someone else at the water cooler.

WATCH WHAT YOU SAY, DO, OR E-MAIL

A by-product of the wonderful era of technology in which we live and work is that Big Brother and the attorney general are always watching what we say and do. We're all familiar with that little bit of the Miranda Rule—you know, anything you say or do can be held against you in a court of law (as the firm's compliance officers will hammer into you every quarter). Part of your work habit will be to watch what you do, what you say on the phone, what you commit to writing, or what you send out via e-mail to colleagues or clients. Remember, Wall Street firms routinely tape phone conversations on trading floors and deal-related meetings, and archive electronic files and e-mails as part of the nightly "disaster recovery" batch process. Ouch.

This self-censorship is a bit tough at first because we're all used to living in a society based on free speech. But the bottom line is clear: in a litigious world, firms that face clients have to be very careful about what they say and do. It's not that what they say or do is wrong, or that they are hiding or obfuscating something—just that any piece of information, however innocent or well intended, can be cannon fodder in the hands of an irate client and a prosecuting attorney. Wall Street is built on reputation and public trust. Those are the crown jewels of any firm, so anything that puts the jewels in harm's way has to be avoided.

So as part of your routine, just think about what you are trying to communicate, both inside and outside the firm. One good test is to imagine that anything you do, say, write, or e-mail winds up—in 18-point bold type—on the cover of the *Wall Street Journal,* or your picture winds up on the morning session of CNBC Squawk Box. You don't need that kind of publicity, so just watch it.

BECOME A GOOD ROAD WARRIOR

Regardless of the job you've landed at the firm, there's a very good chance that you'll be hitting the road, and probably pretty frequently. These days it almost doesn't matter what area you're working in. If you're a banker or institutional salesperson, you're probably on the road 50 percent to 75 percent of the time, but even if you are a controller, risk manager, auditor, or lawyer, you're going to be traveling a lot as well, especially if you work at a global firm with overseas offices and an international client base.

So you've got to toughen up and become a seasoned road vet in a pretty short-time frame. As part of this process, you've got to learn all the ins and outs of corporate travel:

- How to get your admin assistant to make your travel arrangements correctly, the first time
- How to get upgraded to first class on airplanes and into junior suites at the best hotels
- When and where you can "arbitrage" corporate travel policy rules so that you can stay at nicer places (legally)
- How to cut to the front of the line at airline counters, hotel check-in desks
- How to get to and from airports in the most efficient and comfortable way possible
- How to stuff all your gear into one small carry-on suitcase and one briefcase
- What kind of electronic gear (e.g., laptops, pager, Blackberry, PDA, cell phone) is lightest and what kinds of batteries last longest
- How to get an Internet connection anywhere, anytime
- How to get by on two changes of clothes for a one-week trip and never look rumpled
- How to sleep on planes on Friday nights so you don't lose the weekend with family and friends
- How to get the energy and enthusiasm to do the same thing again next week. And the week after that, and so on, for many years.

Hitting the road becomes second nature after a while. The thrill wears off after the second or third outing so you'll have to accept it as part of the job. Don't fight it. Just roll with it, and that will make your routine a bit easier.

KEEP BEING INDISPENSABLE

We've said it before, and we'll say it again, because it is so important to your career: make yourself indispensable. Part of your daily habit should include thinking about the things you can and should do to remain an essential part of what's going on—to make sure that whenever something needs to get done, you get the first call—because everyone knows you'll do it well, efficiently and with good cheer. And remember that part of being indispensable involves coming up with things "out of the blue"—using your own initiative, creativity, and energy to do things that no one has asked for but that serve a purpose and help the firm. So keep at it.

With these habits in mind, let's take a look at how business works at headquarters, at the Big Machine.

The Big Machine: Daily Business at Headquarters

As you spend more time as a productive Wall Street citizen you'll come to know how the business works and how it gets done. You'll figure out who does what, who's important, who holds the balance of power at a particular time, what businesses the firm is really good at and which ones it should just forget about. You'll come to understand how the firm operates on the global stage and how it's perceived in the marketplace. It's like putting together a jigsaw puzzle, piece by piece. You already know what the final picture is going to look like, because you've seen the cover of the box—but it's much more meaningful when you have to put it all together for yourself. That's when you really feel like you understand the dynamics, and mechanics, of Wall Street.

When you're working at headquarters you become very attuned to the rhythm of different business cycles because these determine your own workload and deadlines: daily cycles, which drive trades, deals, crises, and other emergencies; monthly cycles, which influence short-term markets, roadshows, and deal-related activity; quarterly cycles, which revolve around financial reporting; and yearly cycles, which are devoted to performance reviews, bonuses, audits, and regulatory visits. It's always good to know which cycle you, and the firm, are in, so that you know what's going on and what to expect.

THE CENTER OF THE UNIVERSE?

Working at the Wall Street headquarters is unique, like being at the center of the universe. And in a way, you are. You are right in the thick of things, in the middle of the global financial machinery, working on leading-edge deals and important trades that help the world get on with business (but don't let it go to your head—remember the "special people" attitude we talked about in chapter 1).

You'll marvel at how the whole place looks, feels, and functions. The massive, football-field-size trading floors filled with row after row of desks, computers, monitors, phones, hardware, and TV screens, buzzing with energy and motion, the din of phone conversations and discussions punctuated by occasional shouting, expletives, or laughter. Or the discreet, elegant, and hushed banking floors, paneled in deep, rich mahogany and decorated with eighteenth- and nineteenth- century antiques, playing host to important clients and lucrative deals. Or the operations and settlements floors, gritty, spartan, and industrial, dominated by network servers, stacks of paper, and "the cage" (that secure, wire-surrounded room holding all the physical stocks and bonds, a relic of The Street's past), but teeming with frenzied activity. This is the Big Machine.

When everything is working right—the markets are vibrant and business keeps coming through the door—the Big Machine just hums. Of course, when things aren't going well and markets are ugly, it's pretty awful—and you'll see it, feel it, and know it (everything gets very quiet—if you hear an eerie silence on the trading floor, duck your head or run for cover). But remember, through all of the ups and downs at the Big Machine—from the times when everything is great to the times when darkness descends—that the firm is never as great as it seems and it's never as bad as it seems, just somewhere in the middle. It's easy to forget these things in the midst of euphoria or agony, but try—it'll save on the emotional wear and tear.

TRADING AND BANKING:
DIFFERENT WORLDS THAT NEED EACH OTHER

Earlier in the book we talked about different personalities and different job functions. Bankers, traders, salespeople, and staffers are all unique animals, with distinct backgrounds, styles, personalities, motivations, and skills. And they're all necessary. Every function is needed so that the Big Machine can run smoothly. The differences create conflict, but they also demonstrate why Wall Street is special. Where else can you see rough-and-tumble traders shouting at high school-educated salespeople, then shift gears and go into a meeting with polished, Ivy League MBA investment bankers to try and get a client deal done? Where else can you see shy, bookish accountants challenging high-priced trading talent about the price of a trade, or operations clerks refusing to sign off on confirmations because the sales folks made a mistake? These are all different worlds united by a common goal: making money for the Big Machine and making sure the money the Machine makes isn't squandered.

As we've already said, one of the most interesting dynamics exists between bankers and traders. Since many of the deals that bankers source require some type of financing (Function #1), bankers and traders have to work together. For better or worse, they need each other.

Bankers have all the right relationships. They use their polish and charm to see the top brass at client companies and put their negotiating and political skills to work to try and outmaneuver the competition and win mandates. Once they've done that, they turn the business over to the trading desk. It's then up to the trading crew, working with their sales colleagues, to get the deal done. That's where market savvy and instinct come into play: where to price the deal, how to time the market, how to hedge any remaining risk, whom to call to get rid of the last little bits, when to cut and run. These are very different jobs, indeed. In the process, each group thinks that it's the top one, the one that makes the difference. Bankers will tell you that without them there would be no deal to trade. Traders will tell you that without them there would be no one to trade the deal. Personal egos just magnify the differences, sometimes to such horrific proportions that you wonder how they can stand to work together at all.

In reality, neither group is more important than the other. Neither is better or worse. They just have different skills, both necessary to keep the Big Machine running. Though they're different, and don't hesitate to let everyone know that, they both play politics. They go for each other's throats, have shouting matches, complain about who's getting the bigger bonus pool, and give lots of reasons why it's unfair when they're on the short end of the dollars. They basically act like spoiled children. But they never, ever, ever try to blow each other up. Because Wall Street's cycles show that when one group is in the dumps, the other one is there to pull the whole firm through; when one group is ice cold, the other one is on fire. That's really the point: to diversify, so that even when things are bleak somewhere (maybe there's no M&A activity to speak of) the firm can still make it back somewhere else (maybe by printing lots of new stock or bond deals). So, if you happen to be associated with one of the two groups, have your fun, blow off some steam, take some shots at the folks in the other group, but don't stab them in the back, because one day you'll need them to carry your team.

BUSINESS: TO BUY OR NOT TO BUY?

It won't surprise you that Wall Street is into bragging rights. That's because there is a lot to be said for being the biggest, the best, the boldest, the most aggressive, the smartest, or the most profitable. So Wall Street firms try to decide which bragging rights they want and then set out to win those rights—a sort of unwritten corporate goal. They'll do whatever it takes to be thought of as the best in their chosen area (or areas) of expertise. Bragging rights are a great calling card. If you can tell a potential client that your firm is one of the biggest or the best at something, you're almost guaranteed an audience to make a business pitch—and you probably have a better than average shot at winning the business. What client doesn't want to deal with the cream of the crop? And if your firm actually happens to be *the* biggest and *the* best, clients actually start calling, and the firm gets to decide which business it wants to do. Wow.

One of the most important bragging rights is found in the "league tables"—tabulations put out every day, week, month, or quarter that tell everyone who is doing the most financing deals (Function #1), the most M&A deals (Function #3), who's trading the most financial assets (Function #2), who's winning the coveted mandates or making the most money or coming up with the cleverest solutions. These league tables matter because they are a concise reflection of Wall Street power. If the firm can underwrite lots of securities or advise on lots of takeovers in a given quarter, it proves that it is truly a part of the Wall Street elite. If it can repeat the same thing for several quarters—and maybe do the same thing in a few other areas—then it becomes a force to be reckoned with.

Since league tables convey bragging rights, and bragging rights draw in clients like bees to honey, they are ridiculously competitive. To be in the Top 5 or Top 10 of any major league table category is a real accomplishment—meaning everyone on The Street is trying to slit everyone else's throat to occupy one of the Top 5 or 10 slots. So if the firm is serious about climbing in the league tables it has to be very aggressive about getting business. In addition to sending all the high-powered bankers out on the road 24/7, year round, it may also have to take out its checkbook and pay for business. This doesn't mean really writing a client a check, of course, but it all amounts to the same thing.

Think of it this way: if a company wants to raise a $100 million loan and the #1 Wall Street bank is willing to do it at a rate of 5 percent plus fees, the aspiring upstart firm, hoping to win more mandates, may offer to raise the same money at 4.90 percent plus fees. Maybe that's below its own cost, so it loses money. "No matter," the firm's executives think. "If we do this deal, then the client will send us more business in the future, including some of those juicy M&A deals" (the ones with the huge fees that will more than cover the cost of this loan). And as the upstart firm wins more loans, it'll jump up in the league tables, and then clients will be calling the firm, instead of the other way around. So, the argument goes, buying a little league table business can be a good strategy. Maybe, but only if it leads to business that actually makes money. Imagine the Big Machine taking out its checkbook every day to buy yet another deal, another loss leader. If it keeps doing this it may climb from #20 to #12 to # 7, bleeding red all the way. The firm will eventually wind up in the graveyard (maybe as it receives its year-end award for having made the Top #3, in a fitting twist of Pyrrhic irony), so it better know when to say "when." (Note for non—investment bankers: if you really want to irritate a banker sometime, ask him or her how much of the business coming in is due to skill and talent and how much is from the Big Machine's checkbook.) Don't think buying business is reserved for the upstarts. Well-entrenched firms need to do it to keep their #1 or #3 or #5 rankings in the areas of choice. Just remember that if a firm is buying business all the time, it probably won't rank at the top of the one league table ranking that really counts: profitability.

EVERYTHING STOPS WHEN THE DEAL IS RED HOT

Wall Street revolves around deals, and a good part of the daily, weekly, and monthly cycles center on these deals. The bigger the deal, the bigger the excitement, until there is a fever pitch running through the trading floor and the investment banking department (and sometimes even the executive suite, if the deal is big enough). Big deals mean big fees, good publicity, and a boost in the league table rankings—and all of those things help build up the year-end bonus pool. So when a deal surfaces and starts building to its red-hot closing stage, everything else stops. Projects, presentations, roadshows, travel, interviews—nothing matters except making sure that the deal closes on schedule, so it's all hands on deck.

This doesn't really apply to daily trades or small mergers of stock deals. This relates to the "monsters"—a massive block trade or acquisition that lets a desk or department make its whole budget in one shot; a hostile takeover that's been in the works for 18 months; or, a huge, risky loan destined for some emerging nation. These are deals that the firm can't screw up. If you're working on one of these monsters, take it very, very seriously and give it everything you've got; prepare to sacrifice plans, sleep, and weekends in order to help the deal close. If you're not directly involved, but you're affected because everyone else has run off to help, just grin and bear it. Whatever you need can wait till the monster is safely in bed.

GOING ELEPHANT HUNTING

Every so often a posse of bankers or institutional salespeople lands the big one—the huge deal, the one that everyone on The Street has been drooling over (and the one that leaves them all green with envy/purple with rage when they hear someone else has won it). It's the deal with enough juice in it to let the unit, department, or division make its entire budget in one go. When it happens, it's a great moment at the Big Machine.

At the beginning of the year, it's pretty common to see the heads of banking, trading, and sales doing some intensive strategy work, identifying which megadeals are up for grabs and how they can be won. This is big-time elephant hunting: figuring out where the big game is, how to stalk it, and what kind of guns and ammo are needed to take it down—before the folks down the block do it. Like any good safari, there's lots of planning involved:

assembling the right team of relationship managers and salespeople, product experts, traders, and researchers (it may even call for parachuting in the CEO or president), doing preparatory analysis and research, mobilizing resources and coordinating schedules. There are also lots of front-loaded costs associated with trying to win these trophies: the time of the high-priced banking talent, travel and entertainment, pro bono groundwork and presentations, hardware, software, phone time, air time, you name it. When all the preparations are finally ready, it's off on safari, to try and shoot a few.

There's a lot at stake in elephant hunting for both the winners and the losers. For winners it's all about publicity and dollars. Taking down big game means glowing press articles and year-end industry accolades—so many that the firm basks in PR glory for months afterward (and all that publicity attracts many unsolicited clients—those keen to side with a proven winner). The dollars are, of course, huge: the fees cover all the up-front costs and do wonders for revenue and budget targets (and bonus pools). But aiming at a charging bull elephant and missing is awful. The firm gets gored: sunk costs that can't be recouped, irate senior executives with egg on their faces, very public floggings in the press, booing and razzing on the trading floor, and laughter from the firm down the block that bagged the prize. You'll know when the hunters have returned from safari without any bounty: they're all bruised, beaten, bloodied, and crestfallen, and somebody usually winds up paying for the missed shots. In fact, the stakes in elephant hunting are so high that some firms choose not to go out on safari at all, preferring the relative safety and tranquility of going into the back yard to take down lots of little rabbits and foxes, and other relatively benign creatures that can't hurt you if they get away.

THOSE LOVELY BEAUTY CONTESTS

Clients know that Wall Street is a pretty small, competitive place, where everyone's trying to eat everyone else's lunch. So when they need help—maybe some financing or M&A advice—they just call up *every* Wall Street firm and let it "slip out" that a "competitor down the block" has submitted a "very interesting proposal." That gets the wheels turning. When everyone knows everyone else is competing to win the client's business, they give it their all, so the client gets to see all kinds of good ideas and gets great attention and service.

With this sort of competitive business the firm has to do lots of prep work, spend lots of time on the road, and do lots of spoon feeding and hand holding—explaining how things work, why the firm's deal is better than anyone else's, and the great long-term relationship that can develop between the two organizations if the firm gets the mandate—but there's no guarantee it'll win the business. (Little wonder that Wall Street firms love those noncompetitive, "take it, it's yours" mandates that come along once in a while). This can go on for weeks, sometimes months and, as decision time draws nearer, the client usually winds up with 10 or 15 solid proposals to choose from.

Then it's time for the beauty contest. An event that's a bit cheap and tawdry, because the firm really has to put it on the line and deliver the goods if it wants to win, but that's the game. During the beauty contest the client narrows the field of 10 or 15 attractive candidates (deals, usually pitched by the relationship managers) down to three finalists and calls each one back for a final look (i.e., deal structure) and a final question (i.e., the economics of the proposal, aka "how tight can you price the deal and/or how much can you shave your fees?"). Then there's a bit of last-second primping and preening among the finalists, they get out on the runway, show their wares one more time, and the client crowns a winner. Another lovely contest has comes to a close (the product specialists, traders, and salespeople turn up after the show to make sure the deal actually happens so that the firm gets its fees). Then the beauty queens move on to the next show.

THE WHITE-KNUCKLE MOMENTS

Part of life at the Big Machine centers on "white-knuckle moments"—times and events that represent the peak of tension, anxiety, and nervousness. These are usually very unpleasant periods because, even though they may lead to something very favorable (like winning a big deal), the atmosphere is so thick with uncertainty that people actually feel physically ill. Somehow, time always features prominently. There's either too much time (e.g., everyone is waiting around for the phone to ring with news) or not enough time (e.g., everyone is in a mad panic trying to get something done before the deadline hits or the market closes). So what are some of these white-knuckle moments?

Too much time:

- Waiting to hear the final result of the beauty contest on the deal that everyone on Wall Street has been trying to secure for the past year.
- Waiting to see if the brave banking hunters have returned from safari with the much-coveted government privatization/restructuring/financing program (i.e., a really big, and exceptionally rare, elephant).
- Waiting around to hear whether the courts will torpedo a client's hostile takeover attempt (and torpedoing, along with it, the firm's 18 months of hard work and $100 million in success fees).
- Waiting to hear whether the recent regulatory probe into alleged wrongdoings will bring any sanctions and bad press.
- Tallying the final revenue and expense numbers at year-end to see if the firm beat its budget and market expectations.
- Waiting around for your boss to call you into his office to tell you (a) whether you got promoted to managing director or (b) the size of your bonus.

Too little time:

- Winning a multibillion dollar block trade and having to sell it all out in the next 30 minutes—before the market knows the firm owns it (and piles up against it to drive the price down. Nice guys.).

- Doing a spectacularly large client trade 10 minutes before market close on a Friday afternoon before a long weekend, and trying to get rid of all of the risk during that 10-minute window.
- Getting stuck with a bad stock or bond position when a client walks away—hours before the quarter-end reporting period—and realizing that there's no quick way to get rid of it without a big miracle or a big loss.

There are other moments, of course, but you get the point. All anyone cares about during one of these episodes is for it to be over. Now.

WHEN EVERYTHING IS WORKING
IT'S A BEAUTIFUL THING

When everything is working at the Big Machine—when the firm is "firing on all cylinders"—it is truly a marvel to behold. When all of the firm's business lines hit their stride simultaneously, serious money starts flowing in. You can almost hear it sweeping in through the front door. It's a bit like having a printing press down in the basement printing off hundred-dollar bills at a breakneck speed, nonstop, 24 hours a day—you can actually feel the money being made. And the knock-on effects are just as enthralling: press reports about the company gush with admiration, the stock price hits new 52-week highs, thoughts of the year-end bonus pool have everyone walking around with permanent smiles—from July onward. There's an electric feeling down on the trading floor, there's a buzz in the normally hushed mahogany hallways of the banking floors. Even the accounting department is filled with mirth, something totally out of character.

All of this happens when the markets are healthy and the firm is doing what it's supposed to be doing—when bankers start winning good deals (including a few elephants), beat out the competition and climb up the league tables; when institutional salespeople land important new mega-accounts; when traders handle record volumes of flow, and put together some clever (read profitable) trades that dazzle clients and competitors; when the retail sales force hits all-time highs for new account openings. In other words, Function #5 from chapter 1 . . . everything, all at the same time!

That's when it's really fun being on Wall Street, fun being part of the Big Machine. That's when you really believe that global capitalism works and that the firm is making it work (you know, the "special people" feeling). Enjoy these moments—firing on all cylinders doesn't happen very often, so savor it.

WHEN THINGS FALL APART, WITCH-HUNTS BEGIN

Unfortunately, the flip side rears its ugly head from time to time. Things just fall apart. The nice rhythm that carried the Big Machine through a few strong quarters (even years) is no longer smooth and effortless. The breathing becomes more labored, and hitting the right stride gets tougher and tougher. The Machine usually gets it right, but when things start falling apart at the seams—maybe a few deals blow up or go to the competition, some trading desks lose more money than they should, regulatory infractions are discovered, or broader markets go belly-up—the dark side takes over. These are the times you find yourself wishing you were living the simple life in the backwoods of Maine, far, far away from Wall Street. That's because it gets really ugly.

Witch-hunts and kangaroo courts become the order of the day as executive management, in its need to assuage embarrassed board directors and irate investors (and to silence the press), has to look proactive in rooting out the source of the problem(s). Let's face it, if something nasty happens on their watch, they look sloppy and irresponsible, and will almost certainly get a zero knocked off their bonus checks at year-end. And they certainly don't want to lose that zero.

These witch-hunts are at once fascinating and frightening. Fascinating because you get to see senior executives in a mad panic, looking nervous, upset, and decidedly out of control—something very unusual indeed. Frightening because you don't really know what they'll end up doing. They might fire lots of people, including senior level executives; they might close down a business or branch office; or they might slash the bonus pool. Frightening, also, because witch-hunts are often conducted by folks who don't always understand what the business is all about—senior auditors, lawyers, or accountants acting under "executive authority" granted by the CEO or president. They're probably very good at their daily jobs, but they may not be equipped to properly interpret the information that surfaces during a tense investigation—which means if they find something questionable, they may make accusations before they really understand what's going on. Unfortunately, by that time they have probably poisoned the well, ruining someone's reputation and career.

Even though you don't think witch-hunts can affect your daily life, they do. The tension is palpable, and the fear is real, and concentrating on business becomes difficult—everyone is more interested in hanging out by the water cooler to discuss the latest damage, how many are going to get fired, and how much of a haircut the bonus pool is going to take. So witch-hunts have to be taken seriously—you can't really relax until a few sacrificial bodies have been delivered to regulators or shareholders. Then the storm clouds slowly lift, and it's on to do more business—until the next one.

POSTMORTEMS ACCOMPANY EVERY WITCH-HUNT

After a witch-hunt has concluded, the forensic specialists are called in to do their postmortems. These are a favorite pastime of accountants, auditors, lawyers, controllers, and risk managers, who get to put their talents to full use—inspecting the damage caused by the latest blow-up, doing a full autopsy, writing up detailed reports and delivering them to the executive committee (and, if serious enough, the audit committee of the board of directors). The postmortem is a way of documenting what went wrong, assigning blame, and recommending follow-up actions so that the same thing doesn't happen again (let's face it, if the firm steps on a land mine that winds up costing lots of dollars, it better do something to find the other land mines—think of it as a very expensive lesson that everyone had better learn from). The postmortem report becomes part of the permanent record of the firm, and a little something that regulators may look into next time they come visiting. They always like to see whether changes recommended by the post-mortem team have been enacted; often they haven't, because once the witch-hunt and postmortem are completed and someone's head has been delivered on a platter, people lose interest and move on to the next deal or crisis. So regulators typically wind up fining or sanctioning the firm, adding insult to injury.

Postmortems are painful if you're in the line of fire, because you'll have to spend time with the examiners answering detailed questions about how things work, your involvement, what you could have done better to avoid the problem, and whether or not you should be culpable. Even though you may not have done anything wrong (assuming you haven't), you'll still feel like your credibility is at stake. You'll almost feel like bringing in your lawyer and pleading the Fifth Amendment. These are times you don't really like the firm much at all.

THE CASH COW THAT GETS NO RESPECT

We mentioned earlier in the book that retail salespeople who sell securities and advice to the common man and woman are often called the "great unwashed." That should be enough to tell you that they don't get any respect from their institutional Big Machine colleagues. Indeed, their two worlds are far, far apart. We already know that institutional folks position themselves as sophisticated architects of financial solutions for savvy clients—in the trenches, wrestling with the markets and do-or-die deals, the elephant hunts, the beauty contests.

The retail folks have no such pretensions. They know their world is pretty mundane, centered on trying to convince Moms and Pops to shift their brokerage accounts and IRAs over to the firm so that the Big Machine can sell them some more bonds, stocks, and financial advice. Since retail brokers have no illusions of grandeur (actually, they often have inferiority complexes), how on earth can they possibly command the respect of bankers, traders, and institutional salespeople? They can't, and don't even try.

That's really a shame, because the retail business is usually a good one: steady growth and handsome profits. No blockbusters or big game, just a regular ringing of the till. When the Big Machine has an army of retail salespeople around the country, working in little branch offices on Main Street, it's got a ready network for selling all of the new stocks and bonds the bankers are bringing in. That makes winning the deals easier for the bankers, and getting rid of them easier for the traders. Since Moms and Pops usually wind up paying relatively generous commissions for getting in and out of securities, the revenues are good. Retail salespeople also usually push other value-added advice, like estate, tax, and retirement plans, to a client base that keeps getting bigger as the population ages. So they drop even more highly predictable, fee-based revenues to the bottom line. Don't forget, since retail salespeople don't get paid as much as their institutional brothers and sisters, the Big Machine's margins on the whole business are good. All of this can add up to one big cash cow. So if you're not a retail sales rep, give one a pat on the back next time you're walking down Main Street. And if you are, congratulations, keep up the good work.

THE SWINGING P&L

Traders, as we know, are really talented and unique folks with a special set of skills. Good traders know their business well and make money pretty consistently. Great traders know their business extremely well and make lots and lots of money like clockwork (and there just aren't many great traders on Wall Street). But even good and great traders have bad days. You'll know it when you're walking by trading desks and see traders bashing down phone handsets, or kicking garbage cans, or screaming relentlessly at cowering analysts or admin assistants, or putting their heads down on the desks and not moving for a while, or just staring blankly at the flashing screens without moving, blinking, or speaking for 20 or 30 minutes. Give them very wide berth. They are experiencing "swinging P&L" (profit and loss), and they are swinging the wrong way.

The good thing about being a trader is always knowing how much money is being made. The bad thing about being a trader is always knowing how much money is being lost. Real time, meaning now. The trader cannot escape, even for a minute. Even when running down to Starbucks or stopping by the restroom, the trader has a position on the books that is making or losing money. That breeds lots of tension (whether there's "P" or "L"), and either lots of excitement (more "P") or lots of frustration (more "L"). And there are times when the losses are enormous—it may be the markets, a client trade, a bad bet, an ugly hedge, or, heaven forbid, all of them at once. Ouch. In a single day or hour, a trader might undo days, weeks, or months of steady profits—so it's no wonder they sometimes react they way they do. All of this is compounded by the scrutiny. There is no other job in the Big Machine where the results of one's efforts and activities are so quickly (and brutally) put on display for everyone else to see. At the end of every day, everyone knows how much money the firm made or lost in trading, and who made it or lost it. It's tough to be under that microscope, especially when the P&L is swinging into the red. So give these folks plenty of space. They don't need anyone to comment on what's happening. They know it and live it each second of the day and are almost certainly trying to figure out how to make it right. And you'll know the Big Machine's got a great Wall Street trader if he or she can shrug off the red, get refocused, go out, and make it all back.

THE CLIENT ISN'T ALWAYS KING

You know by now that Wall Street business is client-driven. Firms depend on clients for business, business generates revenues, revenues cover expenses and, more important, bonuses. It's a simple relationship that implies the client is the most important thing. The client is king.

But the client isn't always king. Sure, most Wall Street firms like to say that client relationships are their "number 1 priority" (and they may actually believe it and emblazon it on their annual report, corporate principles plaque, and company sweatshirts), but for some the client is really just the means to the end—the end being dollars. If it becomes simpler and easier to earn dollars in some other way—like taking on less demanding or less sophisticated clients, redirecting company assets to other endeavors—then the client will be shown the door, directly or indirectly.

Cultivating and keeping client relationships is expensive. It involves travel and entertainment, giving free access to research and data, cutting fees on some deals or services, and doing a certain amount of pro bono work (e.g., coming up with clever investment banking ideas that might be of interest). So unless a firm can justify the expense by earning enough revenue to cover costs and provide some profit, it may not be worth it. If certain clients are overly demanding (or complain, or threaten trouble), the firm may find that it's just easier to show them the door, sometimes unceremoniously—not quite the way you'd think of treating a king.

In some cases firms might just con their clients—you know, take advantage of their naiveté by selling them something toxic, complex, or inappropriate, things with very juicy fees and probably lots of risk that they have no hope of understanding and that could cause them to lose money. If a few clients explode (Moms and Pops or big institutional customers), who cares, as long as the firm is making money along the way? Believe it or not, that's an attitude some "client-driven" firms actually have. Odd, that in an industry where reputation is the single most important asset a firm can possess, the client isn't always treated like a king. But that's Wall Street.

RAINMAKERS OR THE FRANCHISE?

One of the unique things about Wall Street firms is that they breed, and even promote, the rainmaker system. A system where a few superstars—bankers, traders, salespeople, analysts—can reign supreme at the Big Machine. For a while, at any rate.

Rainmakers are the select men and women who bring in big business on a regular basis. They bag the elephants and do the monster trades that generate millions, tens of millions (sometimes even hundreds of millions of dollars) for the firm. And because they bring in so much money, they are considered The Street's demigods: they have fan clubs within the firm, grace the cover of *Fortune* and *Forbes*, appear on CNN and CNBC, fly on the corporate jet with the CEO, and call their own shots. They're at the top of the compensation pile (usually outstripping the CEO and president by quite a bit, though you won't see that in any of the annual reports or financial disclosure), and they're politically insulated from possible conflict—almost as if surrounded by an invisible force field—so they can carry out their revenue-generating duties without being bothered by nonsense.

But rainmakers, like all mortal demigods, usually have a shelf life. They are elevated to superstar status because they produce, and when they stop producing they become big targets. When a few deals fail to materialize—some elephants go charging down the block to the competition, or some trades go sour—the fan club supporters and yes-men / -women take out their guns and start aiming at the "overpriced" talent. Rainmakers seem never to last for more than a few years—they may hang out at the firm for a long time, but they are unlikely to wear the exalted superstar crown for more than a few years, or a market cycle. Maybe.

Sure, more rainmakers will sprout up, but in the end it's all about the Big Machine and its franchise. If the firm is truly a Wall Street power, the real superstar is in the name and reputation of the franchise, not in the rainmaking abilities of a few bankers or traders. No one person makes the franchise (though one person can certainly help destroy it, through bad judgment, fraud, or worse), but the franchise can make the person. Ultimately, clients almost always want to deal with the firm, with the Big Machine, not the superstar that opens the door and works on the transaction. So even though Wall Street pushes its own rainmakers, it doesn't really need them. It just needs to guard the franchise (as we'll discuss later).

GOOD BUSINESS PAYS FOR BAD BUSINESS, BUT JUST FOR A WHILE

Not every business on Wall Street makes money all the time. That's because markets and clients dictate what's hot, popular, or essential at different points in the cycle. If the economy is strong, maybe M&A activity will increase because clients are feeling confident and want to buy up their competitors. It may mean that investors are buying new stock issues (to finance the M&A deals) rather than Treasury bonds. So the Treasury bond traders may sit around utterly bored, making only tiny profits on the little business that comes their way: the M&A team is basically paying for Treasury bond trading. If the economy is weak, M&A business may fall off, but if interest rates are low, the loan folks may be really active—so the loan desk is paying for the M&A team. This basically means that good, or strong, business has to carry bad, or weak, business. It would be silly for a firm to build up a good M&A or loan or Treasury bond team when the market is hot, make some money for a while, and then shut it all down at the first sign of a "dry spell." In the long run that's a pretty expensive way of doing business, and it shows clients that the firm really isn't committed to the long haul. So a diversified stable of business lets the good business subsidize the bad.

Even this has its limits, though. At some point a firm will decide that it has to get out. If banking deals for auto or pharmaceutical or technology companies look like they're not going to revive for two or three years, it would be foolish to carry expensive bankers, traders, and staff for nonexistent business for so long. So the firm will keep a skeleton crew around to answer the phones but will send out pink slips to the rest of the team. When it looks like an upturn is on the horizon, the firm can hire extra folks, rebuilding capabilities to full strength. Unfortunately, Wall Street firms sometimes get their market timing wrong, meaning they hold off on cutbacks until the month or quarter before the market turns. By the time it's clear that things are getting better, they're woefully understaffed and have probably lost lots of deals to the folks down the block, and they'll wind up paying top dollar to lure talent away from some of their wiser competitors. Bad trade. So timing is everything in trying to figure out how to manage a business over the short- and long-term Wall Street cycles.

SOME BUSINESSES NEVER REVIVE, SO IT'S CUT AND RUN

Some businesses turn sour and never, ever come back. Even though most areas go through some short- or long-term bad patches, they tend to revive—sometimes to full strength (and more) and sometimes only to a modest level, but to one that still justifies the cost of participating. Every so often, though, the Big Machine will see one of its businesses dying on the vine, never to return. So what happens?

Some firms are very active about evaluating the prospects for each of their businesses—basically, figuring out whether they're really moneymakers. Businesses that look healthy get more financial and human resources. Those that look a little bleak may get trimmed back. Those that have zero chance of turning around, even in the long run, may get shuttered. A periodic evaluation is a good discipline to have because it keeps the firm from throwing good money after bad.

Unfortunately, some firms just don't have the discipline. They keep trying to breathe life into a dying business—one that ought to be buried with dignity. They insist on remaining active, a token player in a marginal market, one that's probably bleeding profusely. Why? Maybe because senior management is married to the idea, maybe because it has some "sentimental corporate value," or maybe because there are deeper ties and relationships that forbid anyone to upset the apple cart. That's all well and good, and possibly true and justifiable in some ethical or human sense, but if the economics aren't there and are never coming back, the Big Machine needs to cut and run. As soon as possible.

WALL STREET STRATEGY: AN OXYMORON

Speaking of cutting and running, the Big Machine is good at many things, including the five functions we talked about in chapter 1, but it's not good at strategy. Wall Street and strategy do not belong in the same room. They do not belong in the same sentence.

The Big Machine reacts to markets. That's no surprise, since there are lots of market-sensitive folks running around doing business and managing the firm's fortunes. That's fine for things like trades and deals and client calls, but it's not fine for broader strategic issues, like expanding into new businesses, products, or markets, or developing new relationships and high-level client contacts. These are very critical public issues that require thought, due diligence and, most of all, commitment (and The Street is a bit afraid of commitment).

Strategic issues can't be treated like a market-based "flavor of the month" project. However, often they are. For instance, a firm may declare that it is creating a "strategic expansion" into a new market—maybe opening a new office in Asia, forming a joint venture with a partner in Europe, acquiring another firm in South America, buying the retail operation of a competitor down the block—so that it can capture some of the hot business opportunities of the month/quarter/year. This happens when the markets are strong, management is feeling frisky, and revenue growth is the order of the day. It may also happen when the folks down the block have just announced a similar strategy. Since this occurs only when markets are good (no one opens a new office abroad or buys up another firm when the sky is falling), the premium paid to expand is usually pretty hefty. It's kind of curious that all the savvy traders at the Big Machine don't buy at the top of the market, but executive management usually does. Maybe the people upstairs need to spend a bit of time down on the trading floor.

So what happens when the deals dry up, a crisis rocks the market and disrupts business flows, or the supposed revenues and margins that were the cornerstone of the initiative just aren't there (e.g., someone's assumptions about potential business were just a bit too rosy)? The firm pulls back or pulls out—it abandons its strategy, usually at a considerable financial and public cost. The firm gets lambasted by the press, the partners, the local marketplace, and the shareholders. It has overpaid (again) and proven that it's just not committed for the long haul (again). So prepare to grimace a bit when the CEO announces during one of the quarterly employee update sessions that there's a new strategy in the works (and, no, you cannot short the firm's stock).

FAST TIMES MEAN FAT TIMES

When things are good on The Street, they are good at the Big Machine. Street firms, for all their skill in stringing together deals and booking revenues, are notoriously bad at controlling costs. When the sun is shining and the money is pouring in, anything goes. Executive management loosens the purse strings, and everyone goes on an orgy of spending: hiring more folks than are needed, bringing in consultants to fix little problems or work on nice-to-have-but-definitely-unnecessary projects; handing out free Starbucks cappuccinos on the trading floor every day; spending lavishly on travel and entertainment (e.g., changing the policies to allow folks to stay at the best hotels, dine at the best restaurants, and always fly first-class or business); giving the green light to limo service; upgrading everyone's PCs, workstations, laptops, mobile phones, Blackberries, and PDAs (even though the current ones are just a year old); holding lots of strategy "offsites" (like three-day junkets in very sunny, sandy, exotic locales, thousands of miles from the Big Machine, with just 15 minutes of attendance-optional business presentations every morning); redecorating the executive suite and investment banking floors; replacing the firm's fleet of Gulfstreams; and buying up some little competitors.

These fast times, when money is being coined nonstop, are fat times. That's hardly surprising, since Wall Street never does anything by half steps. So the fatter, the better, until the firm's costs are bursting at the seams. Discipline is nowhere to be seen; spending becomes as important as earning revenues. The stronger the market cycle, the more frenzied the spending.

All these excesses pile up because everyone thinks someone else is picking up the tab—you know, the poor shareholders. Wait a minute. Don't many of the folks at the Big Machine own shares and options? Yep. And, don't some of the Big Machine's top brass own *lots* of shares and *lots* of options? Yep. So aren't they just stealing from themselves? Yep. Go figure.

And these fat times go unchecked until business turns a little sour. When it gets really sour, meaning revenues aren't coming in but cash is still going out at a very rapid rate, executive management sends out cost-cutting memos to stanch the flow of excess a bit, but mostly to be able to tell the outside world that it is "firmly focused on bringing its cost base under better control." Until then, let the good times roll.

ACCOUNTANTS ARE IN CHARGE EVERY QUARTER-END

Accountants are normally quiet, unassuming, cerebral folks who slave away diligently, day after day (and night after night, such is their dedication), at debits and credits, balance sheets and income statements, P&L reconciliations and reserves. All a bit boring, but important. Then comes quarter-end, and these numerate men and women transform. *They are in charge.*

For two weeks before the end of every quarter, accountants basically run the firm—because the financial statements that they put together have a huge influence on the firm's credibility in the marketplace and with investors, creditors, and regulators. Whatever they decide to do— however they interpret accounting rules, and whatever information they put forth—will shape the financial profile of the firm and the price of the stock. Their role is especially critical when they are called on to interpret those gray areas. Since the accounting discipline still has plenty of wiggle room, the accountants, CFO, and external auditors must ultimately decide whether the firm is going to take a liberal or conservative stance on a particular rule. That is, whether it will state *more* or less profit and whether it will make its balance sheet look *better* or worse (legally, of course). Since Wall Street, investors, and credit agencies like "more" and "better," you can see how accountants can have their moments of glory, and they become especially popular around the Big Machine when they pull some kind of rabbit out of the hat to surprise on the upside (or at least avoid surprising on the downside).

Accountants also carry tremendous power at year-end, because the revenue and expense figures that they tally for each business, and then report up to executive management, have a direct bearing on the size of the bonus pool, and that's important to every person at the firm. So when you see those quarterly dates coming up, give the accountants your help and attention. They deserve some assistance and respect at least a few times every year.

EXCRUCIATING YEAR-END FICTION #1: BUDGETS

The Big Machine loves budgets that tell management how much the firm is supposed to make and spend, how many clients it's going to add, how many new deals and fees it's going to book, and, most important, how big the bonus pool is going to be. That's not too surprising, as big organizations need some kind of order. If you've got thousands of folks running around doing business and spending money, you've got to keep track of it all.

Sadly, there's a fiction involved—an excruciating, time-consuming fiction—known as the year-end budget process. This is a process that typically consumes hundreds of accounting man-hours and several tons of paper, and leaves people with frayed nerves and bad attitudes.

It goes like this: during the last quarter of the year, executive management assembles all of the business unit and corporate staff heads to review what they've done during the year—basically, how much they've made and how much they've spent. So it's producers and staffers, revenues and expenses. Then they try to figure out how much they're all going to make and spend the next year.

For revenues, each business unit head gets a budget target for next year that is x percent bigger than this year's. The business unit heads will, of course, protest. Even if they believe they can hit the target, they'll try and lowball the figure, so that if they wind up making the original bogey, they'll look like heroes and get paid more. Think of it this way: executive management says investment banking, which made $700 million this year, has to make $1 billion next year (where that extra $300 million is to come from is, and remains, a mystery. Pixie dust.). The head of investment banking knows that her team can deliver $1.1 billion based on the pipeline of future deals. But she protests, very loudly, about excessive competitive forces, understaffing, lack of travel budget, shaky markets and concludes that the best she can deliver is $800 million. After much discussion, management grudgingly agrees, and $800 million becomes the official target figure. Fast-forward to next year, as bonuses are about to be decided. In walks the head of investment banking with her actual revenues of $1.1 billion, exactly what she thought she could deliver (but didn't bother to tell anyone) and $300 million more than the agreed budget. Wow. She's a star, she beat her budget by almost 40 percent, so she'll get paid very, very well. There are two important points in this (and every other) budget example. The x percent increase sought by executive management is not grounded in reality (it's pretty much a number out of thin air), and neither is the lowball figure provided by the business head (it's pretty much out of thin air, too). So all the budget numbers are fictional. The only folks who probably know what can realistically be achieved are the business unit leaders, like our head of investment banking, and they aren't talking. Why should they? Better to manage the information on need-to-know basis, and executive management doesn't need to know.

Then there's the expense side. Management, regardless of any budgeted growth plans or new initiatives, will always demand that corporate staff expenses be reduced by x percent (again, a fabricated number). Since corporate staffers don't bring in any revenues, they have less room to maneuver than their banking, trading, and sales colleagues—meaning that the best they can hope for is to walk out of the budget meetings with costs flat to last year, despite all the planned growth. So you know something will have to get squeezed along the way.

All of this means that budgets are basically fiction, a classic case of form over substance, which may be okay when markets are strong, as the money keeps pouring in. Everyone exceeds fictional targets, everyone looks like a hero and everyone gets paid. But what if things turn bad or get really, really nasty? Don't worry, if the firm starts sliding behind budget, there's usually a "readjustment." With the stroke of a pen, everyone's budget gets whacked back to reflect the "new market dynamics of the challenging environment" and all of those little minus signs next to the over/under budget figures disappear, meaning the bonus pool is safe. What a relief.

WHEN REGULATORS SHOW UP, HARMONY REIGNS

We know that Wall Street firms have lots of different characters that don't see eye-to-eye on much. Traders, salespeople, bankers, and controllers can hardly be expected to get along. There is a certain amount of natural tension in the daily interactions between all of these groups—tension that manifests itself in the form of rudeness, shouting, or worse. That's Wall Street life. But there are two times when harmony reigns supreme at every firm: when everyone is in a celebratory mood at the headquarters holiday party (after having received very handsome bonus checks, of course), and when regulators walk in the door.

Part of the ongoing life of any Wall Street firm is the planned or "surprise" visits by regulators. These are the federal or state government officials who are supposed to figure out if each firm is doing what it's supposed to, adhering to all the rules and regulations, sticking to internal policies, weeding out problems, disciplining "evildoers," and so on. The worst thing a firm can do is give regulators the impression that all is not well, that there is confusion, chaos, mistrust, misinformation, or anything else that could threaten the smooth operation of the Big Machine. If regulators think there's something wrong, the three-person team of junior regulatory examiners will almost instantly turn into a 50-person SWAT team of forensic auditors, controllers, and operations specialists. As they start digging in deep—really deep—it means more time is wasted, more problems are likely to be uncovered, and more money will be needed to fix things. The firm could get slapped with penalties or fines, and bad press could leak out.

None of this is good. It creates headaches for executive management and board directors, and since no one wants these folks to have headaches, it has to be avoided at all costs. So during these regulatory visits you'll find the Big Machine becomes a chameleon. When regulators walk through the front door, they'll see bankers, traders, accountants, and risk managers all working in harmony as if they were lifelong friends, partners, and colleagues. Everyone will answer the regulators' questions in the same way—almost as if they were reading from the same script (which they are, of course, as they will have been prepped by internal counsel, who take great pains to make sure everyone is saying the same thing in the same way). Everyone will praise everyone else's diligence in running a tight ship and try to present a picture of a firm in which all parts are in lockstep on important matters. In short, everyone lays it on thick, really thick. Then, when the regulators have packed up their work papers, it's back to the same old ways.

The head office experience is unique. It's what Wall Street is all about. Even so, there's more to Wall Street than what happens at the head office. Banks with global aspirations have overseas offices, some very large and very important. There, you have to deal with a whole separate set of issues.

CHAPTER SEVEN

The World Outside: Overseas Business and Postings

Imagine that you're in the daily swing of things at the Big Machine, and your boss invites you into his office one day for a "private chat." Your mouth goes dry, your palms start to sweat, and your heart beats a little faster. You wonder if you screwed up on something. Was it that little mistake on the last trade? Was it the botched sales call? Something worse?

The tension builds, to the point that you feel nauseated.

Then your boss drops the bomb: "How would you like to go to our [Tokyo/Hong Kong/Singapore/London] office for a few years?"

You become dizzy and flushed. "What?! What did I do wrong?" you think to yourself, panicky.

Relax, you haven't done anything wrong. In fact, you've probably done something right. You should view an overseas posting as an opportunity, even as a promotion, not as sign that you're getting "put out to pasture" or being relegated to the minor leagues. As important as the Big Machine is, not everything the firm does revolves around business at headquarters. There's a whole world of deals out there, and if you're being asked to go work in one of those international offices, the firm will wind up paying a lot for your transfer, your housing, and your daily living. So if you were really getting put out to pasture, do you think the firm would pay handsomely for you to occupy a valuable seat in a vital foreign operation? No, it would just fire you. Senior management isn't that stupid.

So what should you do?

It's easy. Sign on the dotted line, pack your bags, and get on the plane ASAP. Time's wasting. You can deal with personal issues (e.g., spouse, significant other, kids, house) when you get to where you're going.

Why? Because, even though it's not commonly known, you are actually striking the mother lode. This is one of the few great opportunities you'll have to make your mark professionally and live very well at the same time.

THOSE OUTPOSTS MATTER

The firm's foreign outposts matter because banking is an international business. Wall Street is part of a global financial network that spans the major centers of the world: Tokyo, Hong Kong, Singapore, London, Zurich, Sydney. If you work for an international firm, its presence in those places is important because there is real business to be done. Lots of the key mandates and the marquis deals come from foreign shores. Lots of the Big Machine's clients live and work in other countries. And some of the best elephant hunting happens far, far away from lower Manhattan. So there's plenty of reason to try to build and support these outposts. Done right, they become more arrows in the Big Machine's quiver, more chances to earn revenues and diversify business.

Winning the business isn't easy, and that's part of the challenge and the fun. You have to crack into the local markets and persuade clients to make use of your firm's expertise rather than the expertise of the bank down the block that's been calling on them every day for the past 20 years. That means trying to understand how business is done—in different languages, in different ways, with different customs, through different laws—and then doing it better, in a way that suits the local market. This is not about taking the Big Machine's template and laying it on top of the local scene. Not only will that not work—it'll probably so offend some clients that they'll never speak to the firm again.

It's also about remaining committed. If the Big Machine wants quality, repeat business, it has to show everyone that it's there for the long haul, and one way of doing this is by keeping a real physical presence for many, many years. There is no room for the Wall Street strategy oxymoron we talked about in the last chapter. Get in and stay in, or just stay away. Talk is cheap. Overseas clients don't want to hear about long-term local commitment from the talking heads back at headquarters, only to have the office pack up and leave when the Big Machine has to trim costs.

That means when you go abroad, you'll be helping the firm make sure that its foreign outposts remain important—by figuring how to do business and figuring out what business to do, and by making sure the place doesn't blow up in the process (you know, that tendency to play with very sharp scissors when Mom's in the other room). In short, you need to make sure that the firm's foreign presence continues to matter, because in this very global and borderless world, it should matter.

YOU GET TO BE YOUR OWN BOSS

What's it really like when you're thousands of miles away from the Big Machine, from the frenzy, excitement, tension, politics, and intrigue? In a word: great. Within a week of hitting the ground you'll realize that your responsibilities have just multiplied rapidly and dramatically. You become your own boss. Sure, you may have some local manager that you report to, but if you're an expatriate transferred from head office, you're probably representing some function (meaning your "real boss" is back home) or you're part of a very small team (meaning you're more senior than you would be back home. This is true even if you're sent over as a senior-level associate or assistant vice president).

Either way, you'll feel that you've got a great deal more authority than you did back home, making decisions that you wouldn't have dreamed of making without prior consultation, taking charge of things, creating your own success. All of this means you have a real chance to distinguish yourself and set yourself apart from your peers back home. Do the job well, on your own terms and through your own initiative, and you will be perceived as mature, capable, and self-motivating back home. Of course, the job pressures are much greater. This is "baptism by fire," because you've got to do things without the safety net you relied on at headquarters. It is now up to you to figure out what to do, how to do it, and when to do it, so that the firm benefits.

But, if you want responsibility and recognition so that you ultimately get more dollars and bigger promotions, *this* is your time and place; this is your Big Thing, one that you don't want to screw up.

OUT OF SIGHT DOESN'T MEAN OUT OF MIND

A common myth that has plagued expatriates for years is that when you leave the Big Machine, you are off the radar screen. Out of sight, out of mind. Wrong. If you are acting as a representative of your department (or are part of the small team) you become the vital link between the outside world and the Big Machine. If anything, the reverse is true. Your 50 colleagues from the analyst rotation are now scattered all over the investment banking department as semi-anonymous M&A or corporate finance worker bees, known only to their bosses (and perhaps their bosses' bosses). You, on the other hand, are the point person in the [Tokyo/ London/wherever] office, working on the big international deals. Suddenly everyone back home seems to know who you are. In this day and age of videoconferences, e-mails, pagers, PDAs, global cell phones, laptops, fat pipes, and wireless networks, you are never out of touch with things happening back at headquarters (the power of telecommunications is made abundantly clear by those regular, 3 A.M. phone calls you get at home from folks in the Big Machine who don't know what time zones are, or just don't care). They know where you are, you know where they are, so you're never off the radar screen. All you really need to do is make sure you schedule an annual return to home base to coincide with the year-end review and bonus cycle (more on this later).

THE JOY OF AVOIDING
ALL THE HEAD OFFICE NONSENSE

A fringe benefit of living overseas (in fact, a benefit that would be worth hard dollars if you could only crystallize aggravation into monetary terms) is avoiding what we might term "head office nonsense" (HON). Every large bureaucracy is plagued by HON. It's the nature of any corporate organization. Lots of this HON can be avoided by simply being out of the country for a good part of the year.

HON comes in lots of different forms. Some of it is benign and well intended, such as new dress code policies, fund-raising drives, mandatory management seminars, and presentations to high school kids. Mild aggravations that you would rather not worry about or be required to do. Some of it is more destructive, such as water-cooler "he said/she said" gossip, promotion and office space jockeying, internecine departmental politics, and so on. This is the more frustrating and time-wasting HON that gets people nervous and upset. So being out of the country as all of this HON churns through the firm is remarkably valuable.

Just because you're abroad, though, doesn't mean you're totally exempt from this sort of stuff. Your regional office probably has some regional office nonsense (RON) going around. But, in any large firm, the size of HON far outweighs the size of RON, so you're lucky.

THE ECONOMICS OF THE OVERSEAS JOB

In addition to the professional angle of being overseas, you've got to pay attention to the personal angle. Some of it's good, and some is bad; sometimes it's interesting, and sometimes it's tough.

When you move overseas with an international firm, you enter a new world. You live well—extremely well—in a way that you never could at the Big Machine. Sure, there are some inconveniences (e.g., language barriers, strange food, bizarre local customs), and you'll probably miss your friends and family. That's only natural, but it tends to pass. Frankly, it passes pretty quickly when you realize how well you're living and how much money you're salting away.

Instead of living in a tiny one-bedroom apartment on the Upper West Side or a suburban house way out in central New Jersey, you'll find yourself living in the middle of a thriving financial metropolis, in a luxury high-rise apartment or a very comfortable house (with 10 times more square footage than you had before—so much, in fact, that half the rooms will still be empty after you've moved all of your stuff in). Everything in the place is new: new paint, new appliances, new furniture.

And the best part of all this luxury living is that it costs you very little. As an expatriate you're entitled to a very generous housing allowance, for which you pay only a "nominal contribution," so you can occupy 5,000 square feet of top-notch, prime space in a luxury building for maybe 25 percent of the rent you paid for that 900-square-foot cave on the Upper West Side. And if you already own a place, the firm usually helps you rent it out and pay the annual management fee—so you just build up equity in your place back home while living the good life abroad. Whatever you wind up saving on housing can go straight into the bank.

You also get a cost-of-living-allowance (COLA) to help defray the expense of living in these expensive cities—yes, some places cost even more than New York. However, by scouting out where the locals do their shopping, planning ahead a little bit, developing some taste for the local cuisine, and figuring out the local transportation systems, you can pretty much bank the whole COLA, which can be as much as 50 percent of your base salary, depending on the city you're living in. Since local housekeeping help is often cheap, you can have a housekeeper that comes in every day to do all those dreaded chores (laundry, cooking, cleaning, shopping, and anything else that sucks up your scarce free time). If you've got kids, their schooling will also be paid for. That's meaningful, because if you're sending them to an international school the tuition is usually exorbitant. Again, a little extra money for your bank account.

Of course, if you take the expatriate option you are normally "tax equalized," meaning you pay taxes on your earnings as if you were still back home. But who cares? You'd be paying them anyway. (And under a "gross up" concept, the company pays the taxes on your housing, COLA, schooling—anything that might be regarded as compensation—so it's not your problem. Sweet deal.) Note that under no circumstances do you want to sign up for the local-hire package. Though you can get a tax break if local taxes are lower than they are back in the United States, you don't get the housing, schooling, or COLA. Bad trade.

The equation is simple: Spacious luxury housing at nominal cost + bankable COLA and schooling + cheap housekeeping = Money ahead and living well.

You're now a bit closer to retirement.

TRAVELING IN STYLE

One of the other great perks about living abroad is traveling often, and in style. We divide these into "home leave" trips and business trips.

Under a typical Wall Street package you get one or two "home leave" trips a year, typically back to New York, but if you can demonstrate that its cheaper for you to go to Telluride or Bermuda or the Maldives, that's okay, too. (If you happen to have spouse and kids, their trips are paid for as well). And you don't have to fly economy on some second- or third-rate airline. You get to go business class (or its equivalent) on a good airline. And after one or two of these trips, you generally have enough miles to upgrade yourself to first class or get free tickets for your friends and family, or take that extra "dream trip" you've always wanted (e.g., the Great Barrier Reef, Tahiti, the Himalayas, Paris and the Wine Country).

Then there are business trips. Don't forget that you've got a job to do while you are abroad, and that means lots of regional and international travel. Though it can be a hassle and can wear you down (remember your road warrior tips), you'll at least be doing it the right way: first or business class (depending on your position and company's policy), taxis or limos on both ends (no "train to the plane" or bus connections), first-class hotels (you know, the ones that always feature in the "Top 10" lists of the travel magazines), fine dining in good restaurants (three times a day). You will do this six to ten times a year, depending on the demands of the job. And then there is the annual return to home office, generally around year-end review/bonus time. Same great travel policy, only this time you aren't going back to your one-bedroom apartment when you land in New York, you're going straight to the Four Seasons or St. Regis, or some similar establishment. And you always get a warm reception when you show up at head office. You are typically greeted by your boss, colleagues and analyst rotation friends as some kind of great warrior returning from the battlefield, having fought valiantly, vanquished the enemy, and secured valuable treasure (e.g., squashed the competition and won some deals). When you do your business traveling the right way, life as a road warrior becomes a bit easier.

With planning and foresight, you'll also find that the miles you accumulate on your business trips are more than enough to cover all the personal travel you will want to do for years to come. You see the world the way it was meant to be seen—with style and for free.

THE PAIN OF CULTURE SHOCK

It's not all peaches and cream, of course. The downside of the expatriate gig is that you're living in a foreign land, far away from the comforts (or perceived comforts) of home, and far away from family and friends. For some, this is a tough adjustment. It's not easy living in a place where the food, language, and customs are alien, and where you sometimes feel isolated and unwanted.

The first three to six months of your assignment are actually enthralling—the cultural and educational dimension of your experience seems unique and valuable. Everything seems exciting, mysterious, and vibrant, and you feel your horizons broadening. You'll even wonder why you were so shocked and scared when your boss first raised the topic—life seems so much more interesting when you're abroad.

But wait. After that six-month "cultural honeymoon" you'll wake up in your luxury apartment one day and wonder what you've actually done. This means the novelty has worn off and culture shock has set in. Things that were new and exciting seem an unpleasant hassle. You'll find that you're wrapped up in a world you don't understand and can't relate to. You are the proverbial "stranger in a strange land," and you just wish you could get back home. If you've got a spouse or significant other and some kids, it's even harder because they're probably going through the same feelings, so everything gets multiplied. You long for things from home: you wish your family or friends could visit you (wait, they can hop on a plane anywhere), you wish you could go to Starbucks for a latte (wait, you can do that anywhere), or watch the Dolphins play some football (wait, you can do that anywhere), or see the new James Bond movie (wait, you can do that anywhere), or go to Virgin Records and get the new U2 album (wait a minute here). Okay, bad examples in this global world. So maybe the things you *think* you need aren't as far away as you *think* they are.

Relax, it'll pass. Accept where you are, enjoy your time, and learn and experience everything you can. Make an effort to be part of where you are.

Don't fight it, and don't wish you were back home. It's much easier that way. Within 12 to 24 months, you'll find that things are okay. The culture shock wears off. You'll have learned how things work, made new friends and developed a network of your own, established a routine that feels comfortable, and, though you probably can't or won't integrate into the culture fully, you'll start to feel more at home. So just enjoy yourself.

AFTER YOUR FIRST POSTING YOU'LL WANT TO DO OTHERS UNTIL YOU'VE DONE THEM ALL

Okay, so you've finished your first expat "tour of duty" after two or three years (that's how long the firm needs you to commit in order to make it economically worthwhile to send you over in the first place). Now what? Well, you need to consider a few things:

- The size of you bank account before and after your expat assignment
- The living conditions you've enjoyed over the past few years versus the prospect of returning to an apartment on the Upper West Side (okay, so you can allow yourself to upgrade to two bedrooms since you've got a few more dollars, but it's still going to be in the same dingy building/neighborhood)
- The places you've seen and things you've experienced while overseas
- The independence you've enjoyed, the professional responsibilities you've assumed, and the goals you've accomplished
- The reduced aggravation and stress levels you've experienced by avoiding Big Machine HON

If you've managed to deal with culture shock and distance from friends and family, then the answer, once again, is easy. Talk to your boss back home, tell her that you are the ideal candidate for that new opening in the [Tokyo/ Singapore/Hong Kong/London/Zurich] office because of your recent overseas experiences, your maturity, and your ability to work independently. You will undoubtedly be able to convince her (especially for Asian posts, which are always a bit harder to fill as a result of distance/culture/language barriers). Then pack your bags and prepare for another adventure. Try to repeat this again in a few years, until you've covered all of the firm's international operations. In a large firm this can be three or four major locations of two to three years each: six to twelve years. Then you can return to head office as a seasoned international financier.

This doesn't mean that if you can't/won't/don't want to go overseas you won't succeed on Wall Street. Of course you can, and will, as long as you work really, really hard and can play the game. Lots of people have done it and do it, and, frankly, not everyone is cut out for the international life (remember, the culture shock can be tough for a while, and working in a smaller regional office means different pressures and responsibilities). But your path will be different. If you stay at the Big Machine, you won't gain the same financial windfall as your expat colleagues, and you won't develop a different business perspective (that much is certain), though you will be in the "thick of things," for better or worse. If you like the pulsing, teeming, organic experience of being in the Wall Street head office (versus the relative tranquility and civility of the regional offices)—if you like being in the middle of the HON, the gossip and politics that are part of the Wall Street character; if you like being close to family and friends and think that New York really is the center of the galaxy; if you can't do without your coffee and bagel from the vending cart outside headquarters—then stay and enjoy.

But be prepared for turbulence, because head office is always the scene of the ugliest bloodlettings and politics.

CHAPTER EIGHT

Fasten Your Seat Belt: Weathering Office Politics and Market Cycles

You've probably started to figure out that even though Wall Street has its moments of fun, excitement, and glory, it's not all sweetness and light. Obviously it's not, and it can't be—this is Wall Street, after all. You'll learn pretty quickly that there are patches of extremely nasty turbulence along the way, so you have to keep your seat belt fastened. Sometimes, when things get really bumpy, you have to learn to put your head between your legs and keep a very low profile until you're safely on the ground again.

There are two different kinds of turbulence that can make Wall Street an ugly place to be: internal (office politics) and external (market cycles). Both are difficult—arguably impossible—to avoid or influence, so the best thing you can do is learn how to cope with them.

WATER COOLER POLITICS ARE RAMPANT, SO DON'T DRINK THE WATER

Office gossip, political intrigue, and destructive rumors are always being hatched somewhere—in the hallway by the water cooler, in the company cafeteria, at the bar during Happy Hour. That is a fact of life in the corporate world, and it's certainly a fact of life on Wall Street. Regardless of your job, responsibilities, or title, odds are that you will someday become the topic of conversation at the water cooler. Analysts, associates, vice presidents, managing directors, the CFO, and the CEO are all fair game for truths, half-truths, semi-half-truths, lies, and egregious lies.

It doesn't matter whether you have or haven't done something, whether you're a good or bad boss or team member, whether you're a nice person. You'll "get yours" at some point—it's just simple probability. Assuming that one new rumor is hatched each day about only one person in the firm (it's probably greater than that, but we're being conservative), and assuming you work in a firm with 2,500 other folks and there are 250 business days per year, sometime in the next 10 years you'll become a target (for ease we're discounting those that enter and exit the firm). You'll walk in to work one day to sneers and chuckles and, after some investigation, find out that you've become the latest focus of gossip. Hope that it's benign, because sometimes it isn't, and things get nasty and out of control (e.g., rumors of intradepartmental romance, nepotism, expense account fictions, travel and entertainment abuses, trade tickets in drawers, mistreatment of clients—real no-no's that can threaten a promotion or bonus, or lead to even worse). Though people should know better, they don't. So just bring your own bottle of water so you can ignore what happens over at the cooler.

THE HIGHER YOU CLIMB, THE BIGGER A TARGET YOU BECOME

Human beings are fundamentally insecure, and Wall Streeters, since they are so important (or think so, at any rate), are supremely insecure. Given this level of supreme insecurity it should come as no surprise that Wall Streeters are always taking shots at each other—and this means taking shots at their colleagues, not just the competitors down the block.

Wall Streeters are very jealous of the professional and monetary success achieved by their peers, so the more success you achieve, the greater the jealousy you stir up in others, and the more likely you are to get shot at. Managing directors, heads of businesses and divisions, investment banking rainmakers, hotshot traders, senior salespeople who dine with politicos and captains of industry, research analysts who appear regularly on CNN and CNBC, are all prime targets. The level of professional success they enjoy (and the highly visible pecuniary success that comes with it, e.g., mortgage-free duplex condos on Fifth Avenue, mansions in Greenwich, beach homes in the Hamptons, ski homes in Vail) brings out the worst in people. If you're lucky and skilled enough to occupy one of these highly coveted positions, you've probably already developed pretty thick skin and are used to the continuous barbs and slings. If you're not quite there yet, but aim to be, start preparing yourself by getting used to the nastiness, backstabbing, and double-dealing—things that are all part of daily life when you're successful within the firm (but things they don't teach you how to deal with when you're going through the regular training program).

By the time you reach the upper echelons of the firm you'll find you spend more of your time dodging bullets than doing constructive business. Your professional contributions become less important than your overall ability to survive the shots. If you are in the "wrong camp" when a new president or CEO is appointed (a bit similar to being a Democratic staffer when a Republican president moves into the Oval Office), you should probably start preparing for retirement. The new seniors will appoint their own people to the prime jobs, and since you have one of the prime jobs and the wrong party affiliation, you're just walking around with a bull's-eye on your suit. It's probably time to go. It's kind of sad that on Wall Street you can get to a level of seniority at which your professional skills and contributions matter less than your connections. But we won't feel too bad for those getting squeezed out. They'll be sipping tropical drinks at their villas in Bermuda or hot chocolate at their chateaus in the Swiss Alps.

THE COZY OLD BOYS' NETWORK AT THE TOP

Let's press on with that last thought by talking about something unpopular, something that some regard as absolutely shocking and positively untrue: Wall Street is still driven by a cozy "Old Boys' network." Who you know, what school you went to, and how you play the game is more important than what you know, what you do, and what sort of character you have. Wall Street is still primarily run by older men, men who have been in the business a long time and have very firm ideas about the way the world works.

We can rail at the unfairness of having lots of old guys in control (especially when they have outlived their knowledge and usefulness and serve in their positions mostly because they have board members in their pockets), but that won't help. Recognize that, in this day and age, the network still exists. Because the network exists, ceilings and barriers exist—for women, for minorities, for those who don't hold a U.S. passport, for those who didn't go to the right school, for those who are too "young and aggressive" for the corporate culture, for those who don't say "yes" all the time. Just look at the pictures in the executive management section of any annual report from any Wall Street firm and it'll be pretty clear. Though there is plenty of talk about diversity, about cross-cultural integration, about pure meritocracy and promoting the true performers, Wall Street has a *long* way to go before we will be able to say that it has successfully integrated and plays fair. Talk is cheap.

So if you don't fit into one of the "acceptable categories" you've got two choices: you can rise to the level of your natural abilities where politics and connections can still be managed and overcome (e.g., maybe managing director, but almost certainly not executive management) or you can fight the system, kicking and screaming all the way. A select few have fought it successfully. Many others have not. Just remember that if you fight and lose, you're finished at the firm, and you may be finished on The Street (funny how word gets around). It's for you to decide how to play it.

GOOD POLITICAL CONNECTIONS
MEAN PAST MISTAKES DON'T MATTER

Politics and the Old Boys' network mean that if you're in the right political camp, past job mistakes don't matter all that much. If you know the right folks you can afford to have a couple of black marks beside your name because the system lets your sponsors gloss over them. Whatever you may have done that wasn't particularly good or nice—maybe you accidentally blew up a client or let some key deals fall apart, maybe you failed to notice some control problems that could have prevented a loss—tends to get insulated and sanitized so that you can carry on with your career. Everyone makes mistakes, right? So why make a big deal of it?

Of course this applies only if you've got good connections. If you don't, or if you are actually in the wrong political camp of the moment, forget it. That's when the past actually matters, and it usually gets magnified to horrific proportions by the other side, so that agitators, or those who might threaten the status quo, get pushed out. Beware.

The only time political connections can't help is when a problem or mistake is so stupendous, so unbelievable, that it brings public embarrassment to the powers-that-be. When the problem gets to be so awful that it's reported on the front page of all the newspapers and the evening news (yes, even your folks know what's going on), then the firm's reputation is at stake. No one gets to monkey with the firm's reputation. That's when the network draws in to protect the tight inner circle, leaving everyone else blowing in the wind. Short of that, though, expect support regardless of what you do—as long as you stay connected with the right side.

DON'T MONKEY WITH THE FIRM'S REPUTATION

Reputation is everything, especially in the financial world. Big companies that actually make things can rely on their physical products to bring money in the door. They have factories, machinery, inventories, a network of suppliers and clients—tangible things that can be touched and felt. Sure, they have to be concerned about their public image, but at the end of the day they can still sell cars or TVs or soda. Not so with services industries, and not so with Wall Street. Wall Street is about nebulous, soft, intangible things like goodwill, reputation, and "doing the right thing." At least that's the intent.

Ultimately, a firm's reputation is its business franchise. If clients trust the firm and its reputation, they'll give it business and help build the franchise. If they don't, it's pretty much over. A Wall Street firm can't fall back on hard assets. Its assets are its people—the brainpower and behavior that its people bring to the table. People make the reputation. Reputation can be damaged quickly, sometimes by the act of just one person, and repairing it might take years and years, if it can be repaired at all. Stuffing trade tickets in drawers to hide losses, completely screwing clients (repeatedly), lying to regulators, and other nasty things like that have buried a few firms over the years.

So in the midst of all the politicking, the seniors will do whatever needs to be done to protect that reputation, that franchise (including sending their allies and compatriots to the gallows, if that's what it takes). As you're carrying on your daily affairs, just remember not to monkey with the firm's reputation. If you do anything that can cause even a temporary dent in goodwill, you're gone.

WHEN THINGS GET BAD, CORPORATE PRINCIPLES GO OUT THE WINDOW

Lots of Wall Street firms have "corporate principles" and "codes of conduct" that they use to help define their characters and beliefs. These generally spell out, in four or five sentences, all the good things that the company stands for—integrity, respect, professionalism, motherhood, and apple pie. These get emblazoned on brass plaques, which are then bolted to the walls in very conspicuous places. The principles are well intended, and they make clients and shareholders feel a bit warmer and fuzzier. Many folks at the firm believe in them and try to follow them, especially if they haven't been through a nasty market downturn. But the more seasoned (jaded? cynical?) members just kind of smirk when they see the principles, and they groan, audibly, when they're forced to attend another corporate session touting them.

Regardless, one thing is always true: when revenues head south, costs head north, profits get squeezed, and bonus pools start to shrink, principles go out the window. That's when all the good talk about respect, professionalism, and integrity vanishes. Everyone's focus turns to keeping his or her job. If that means stabbing a colleague or two in the back, fine. If it means selling a customer something he/she doesn't really need, fine. Anything to get revenues back up, costs down, and the share price back where it belongs.

You'll know things are starting to get bad when maintenance men prowl around the hallways removing all the brass plaques. It's sort of a "leading indicator" of bad times to come. Principles get buried away in the corporate basement when significant layoffs start to occur. If the company is going to fire 20 percent of its workforce, sack a few high-profile deal makers, cut back on customer service in order to shave expenses, and close down an important regional office that the firm is committed to, it doesn't want the principles hanging in the hallways for everyone to see and ponder. Executive management doesn't really want to deal with questions about principles when it is basically flouting a few/some/all in order to get the stock price back up.

But don't worry—when the next bull market cycle returns, the predictable hiring spree begins anew, and the sun is shining again, someone will scamper down to the basement, find the principles, dust them off, and bolt them back onto the walls. Life is good again.

CUTTING INTO MUSCLE

For all of Wall Street's market savvy and technical prowess, for all the time and effort it puts into recruiting, training, rotating, and promoting, it usually falls short in one key area: figuring out how many employees it needs during bad times. It's no surprise that when things start looking ugly—markets fall apart, deal flow dries up, clients go on very, very long vacations—a firm's management pulls out the hatchet and starts swinging, sometimes randomly but always energetically. Heads roll, and it's not a pretty sight. Just how many swings and how many severed heads depend on the perceived depth of the downturn, but it's not an exact science. Downsizing (or, as management is fond of saying, "rightsizing") is one of the risks of working on Wall Street. No one will argue with that (you are, after all, a cliff dweller). When things are lousy, tough personnel decisions have to be made.

Unfortunately, management often doesn't know when to say "when," and cuts far more than it needs to, even in a cyclical downdraft. It may react far too strongly to what will turn out to be a short-term aberration, firing wholesale in a market that comes roaring back just six months later. This means that the firm, as it's swinging away, is probably cutting into muscle, getting rid of the real talent in the organization—the very people who can improve the firm's fortunes—in order to tell the marketplace (you know, shareholders, credit rating agencies, the financial press at large) that it is bringing the cost base in line with the new business realities. It might be saving on costs in the very short-term, but if it has cut too deep for the market cycle then it is getting rid of talented folks who will have to be rehired in six months, when things are good again—and rehired at a higher cost, of course. So if you think your job is safe because you are one of the firm's most valuable assets, think again, because when the hatchet slices into muscle, you're at real risk.

EXPATRIATES: INSULATION VERSUS VULNERABILITY

The great expat jobs we talked about in the last chapter are a bit of a double-edged sword. On one side, you get to avoid a lot of the idle gossip, chatter, and political intrigue that literally flow through the hallways, offices, and trading floors at headquarters—the HON. That means you save yourself a great deal of frustration and aggravation and can stay focused on business. On the other side, you may lack the political connections that your headquarters colleagues enjoy—political connections that give them a bit more insulation when the pink slips start circulating. Because you've got to remember that while you're halfway around the world minding your own business, your colleagues are busy hobnobbing with the political movers and shakers of the moment. As we said, Wall Street is still very much about who you know, who knows you, and whether or not you're playing the game, especially when you reach more senior levels, such as director or managing director. At that point skill, accomplishments, energy, and ideas can take a back seat to politics and political connections. So if you aren't in the political loop back home, you're much more exposed when the firm starts large, wholesale cuts. All of those unknown faces abroad that lack a Big Machine sponsor suddenly look very vulnerable.

SAVING FOR A RAINY DAY

If you're giving Wall Street a shot—becoming a cliff dweller by trading in your job security for a chance to make some serious jack—you should be salting away whatever you can for the day you go sliding down the precipice. The safest, and most conservative, assumption you can make is that you *will* fall of the cliff at some point. If you don't, great, but if you do, you'll be prepared.

As a finance professional you should already understand the value of money and be managing your income and assets prudently. That means sacrificing a few of life's fun things in order to build up a little rainy-day fund. If you live in Manhattan or the immediate environs, the cost of living is expensive, so you've got to plan ahead. Figure out how much it'll cost to live modestly for about a year without a steady source of income. You might think a year of cushion is too much. You're probably thinking that you're talented, have some experience and a good degree, you've successfully rotated through the analyst program and have been promoted to AVP or VP. It won't take a year to find another job if things go sour.

It will. Just remember, if you're a good performer (some of that Big Machine muscle) and still get blown out the door, you're probably in the middle of a large Wall Street downturn, where lots of Street muscle is getting cut. That means all 20,000 or 30,000 or 50,000 experienced Wall Streeters are going to be applying for the same 15 jobs that happen to come up during the quarter. Think about it, and start saving (and, remember, the little goodbye kiss that the firm gives out doesn't usually amount to much, maybe a week of pay for each year you've worked, and some medical benefits lasting a couple of months. Gee, thanks).

SOMEHOW, WALL STREET ALWAYS BOUNCES BACK

The lessons of history are important to keep in mind when things look really bleak—when two-thirds of your colleagues from the analyst program have been fired, your boss has been demoted, your best friend on the mortgage-backed securities desk has just been handed a pink slip, the CEO has just announced that the year-end holiday party has been canceled, and bonuses will be no more than 10 percent of last year's bonanza (if you're lucky). In those dark hours be thankful you still have a job, work like hell, and remember: Wall Street always bounces back. There have been ugly market cycles and bloodlettings in the past from which The Street has recovered, and there will undoubtedly be more in the future from which The Street will recover.

So don't lose faith or confidence. Just try to grin and bear it (*gambate*, or "courage," as your colleagues in the Tokyo office might say). Remember that good times will come around again. If you're committed to a Wall

Street career and can make it through some of the dark days, don't lose faith, and don't abandon all of your hard work in favor of some other career you don't feel as passionate about. Also don't let the experience embitter you. For all of its occasional unfairness and conflict, for all of the politics and nastiness, Wall Street's still an interesting and fun place to be. Take the bad like an adult. Accept it, learn from it, and move on—but not away.

If you manage to weather a few bouts of office politics and one or two market downturns, you are starting to look, talk, and walk like a seasoned Wall Street pro. So how do you take all of that experience and translate it into promotions? Let's take a look.

CHAPTER NINE

Scaling the Mountain: Getting to Managing Director

You've made it through some market downturns and come out all right, you seem to be coping with office politics and, most important, you're gaining experience by making real contributions—doing good trades or deals, landing important new clients, or fixing some corporate problems. Congratulations, again! You are moving in the right direction, and your ultimate goal is that much closer. Your goal, of course, is to get promoted to managing director (or MD, the equivalent of partner in some firms).

On Wall Street, getting to MD means winning the big prize—a prize that is cherished all the more because firms don't hand it out like candy. You've got to have the right stuff, and despite some of the political shenanigans we talked about in the last chapter, you've still got to earn it.

Mortals can, and should, aspire to the rank of MD. As we said in the last chapter, rising higher than that, to executive management, depends heavily on connections and background—meaning almost everyone on Wall Street is unqualified. Since the pool of available executive management positions is extremely small, you're better off trying for MD. You can, of course, aim for the stars—but you may want to first consider a more realistic, and still very attractive, alternative. Don't forget that producing MDs often get paid even more than their executive bosses. So, although they may not get to fly in the corporate jet, who cares? They get the sweet green.

THE TARGET ZONE

So how do you climb that mountain? How do you get to MD, so you can enjoy all of the goodies the job has to offer (while suffering all the burdens, pressures, and responsibilities that accompany the title)? First, let's understand exactly what you are competing for: one of a *very* small number of lucrative, senior-level jobs. Though Wall Street firms are all a bit different, a typical one looks just like a pyramid:

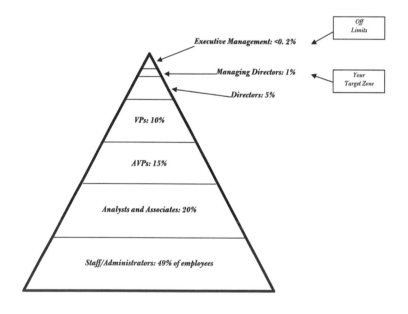

So, in a 10,000-person Wall Street organization, the base of the pyramid might feature 5,000 staffers/administrators—otherwise known as non-bonus eligible personnel—who work hard but don't really share in the spoils the way the rest of the firm does. This group includes secretaries, assistants, operations clerks, maintenance folks, network/PC specialists, cafeteria workers, security guards, and so forth. Above that we might find about 2,000 or so analysts and associates (remember those days?), followed by 1,500 AVPs, 1,000 VPs, and 500 directors. Then comes your target zone: the 100 MD spots (just forget about the two dozen or so executive management spots).

Most firms like to keep these proportions relatively constant, so if the company is growing, the absolute number of MDs is going to expand. Unfortunately, the reverse is also true, especially if the firm is in an extremely cost-conscious mode. That's when expensive MDs lose their heads. (It reads well in the financial press and sits well with investors. Think about it: if you were CEO, would you rather fire 1 ultraexpensive MD that has hit a dry spell or 50 super-hardworking operations and PC specialists who are doing all they can to keep the firm's daily operations going? They cost the same.) So your best bet for getting to MD is when the markets are expanding—try and time your career moves accordingly. But remember, getting to MD is *very, very difficult.* Many try, few succeed. Don't let that dissuade you, just remember that getting into that target zone is tough.

THERE IS A STRICT PECKING ORDER
THAT YOU CAN'T VIOLATE

Like the military, Wall Street has a pecking order—one that can't be tampered with. It has a hierarchy, like the one in the pyramid above, that it enforces very strictly. If it doesn't, chaos reigns. And even though Wall Street firms love chaos in the markets (that's when they make the most money), they don't like chaos in their operations.

So even if you are the most brilliant associate on earth—a Wall Street prodigy, capable of doing the work of a seasoned director—you still have to work through the ranks like everyone else. There is no leapfrogging. You won't see people being promoted from associate to director, or VP to MD, if the pecking order has intermediate titles and roles. Though Wall Street is political, it is also quite strict in making sure everyone goes through the proper steps. True, you may be so good that you get promoted from VP to director after only one year instead of the more typical three to five years—but you still have to make all the stops. So when you are doing your career planning, don't think you'll be doing any title jumping. It's just not the Wall Street way.

DOING YOUR TIME

You've got to be prepared to put in your time in order to get promoted—it's just like having to pay your dues when you're a trainee and then an analyst. Again, you may be the most brilliant young superstar that The Street has seen in a generation, but there are some things that you can know and learn only by hanging around, watching how things work, and living through a few bad spells. Everyone's a star in the roaring bull market, but the real talent shines through during the ugly, sloppy bear markets. These are experiences that you can accumulate only gradually—a sort of financial osmosis. There's no "crash course" you can take to accelerate the process.

Besides, doing your time means becoming more mature. A 25-year-old associate, though really good, say, at highly leveraged acquisition deals or derivatives trading, *generally* isn't going to be as mature as a 32-year-old VP. That 7-year span adds a lot to a person's ability to cope with problems, issues, crises, human relations, and conflict—things that you can't possibly learn in B-school (no matter what the university brochures tell you) or even in the firm's training program. So, even though biding your time may be frustrating, deal with it and make the most of it. Learn and experience all you can, so by the time you're ready to make the jump to director or MD, you'll be equipped with experience that only time can provide.

So, let's cut to the chase: how long will it be till you can make director or MD? Assuming that you are smart, energized, and capable of delivering the goods consistently, that you have some political connections, and that you are working in a market with just a few minor (one or two year) downturns, figure on the following:

Analyst: 1—2 years
Associate: 1—3 years
AVP: 2—3 years
VP: 3—5 years
Director: 3—5 years

That means you'll have to spend at least 10 years, and perhaps 18 to 20 years, to get your shot at MD—if you get a shot at all (remember, time alone does not guarantee promotion on Wall Street, as it does in some other industries). Time, and the experience brought by time, has to be part of your career plan. There's no way around it.

DELIVER THE GOODS
IN AN OBVIOUS AND TANGIBLE WAY

Adhering to the pecking order and doing your time are minimum requirements when scaling the MD mountain. Politics aside, the only way you get to the upper echelons of the firm is to deliver the goods. You have to be good to get promoted. Wall Street doesn't hand out director and MD titles to people who just show up for work, punch the clock, and do only what is expected of them. You've got to travel well beyond that to even be considered for a top spot.

This means that from Day One of your Wall Street career you have to start building a record of success. Remember what we've already said a few times: be indispensable. You have to deliver on things—deals, clients, projects, trades—that really matter, in an obvious and concrete fashion. People around the firm have to associate you with tangible successes like, "Oh, there's Mary Smith. She's very good; she just landed that West Coast M&A deal the firm has been trying to get for two years. And she did it all by herself." Or, "There's John Brown. He's outstanding. He developed a way to reconcile the firm's books and records through a computer interface—and it took him only 18 months." Do a few things like Mary and John, and you'll start moving to the top of the promotion lists.

One important caveat: *never* rest on your laurels. It's been said many times before, and it's certainly relevant here: you are only as good as your last game/win/project/deal/trade/success. People on Wall Street have pretty short memories when it comes to good achievements. It's probably something to do with the trading mentality, where the only thing that really matters was the price of the stock, bond, or deal five minutes ago. Forget about the M&A deal or reconciliation project you completed 6 or 12 months ago. That's ancient history on Wall Street. You always need to be searching for the next set of goods to deliver and deliver them. And then do it again, and again, and again. Be indispensable. Over time, different executives in the firm will know that you've been driving the bus on lots of big things for a long time—and you will be rewarded.

GET PUT IN CHARGE OF A BIG THING AND MANAGE IT WELL

As you progress in your career, you'll eventually come across an opportunity to do something big. Very big. Huge. If you have a proven track record of doing very well on smaller things—individual deals or trades, new client relationships, a control project, a research study—then you should be on the lookout for a Big Thing. A Big Thing is one with firm-wide visibility— one that even the old boys up in the executive suite know about. It's a thing that everyone knows has to get done (or would like to have done) but that no one has actually done. When you spot one (or can create one), make it yours—if you think you are ready. Tell your boss you want to be put in charge. When you complete it (successfully), you'll be on track for MD.

You usually can't put yourself in the running for the management of a Big Thing unless you've been around for a few years. By then, you'll know about how The Street works and how the firm works. You'll know the problems, pitfalls, land mines, and booby-traps you've got to dodge, who you can call on for help and who you can trust, and the political forces that might stand in your way. You can't manage your Big Thing unless you know all of that. This means you're probably going to be a VP or director with enough seasoning and maturity if you're going to have a realistic go at it.

But make no mistake: Big Things are career makers or breakers. You've got to be ready for this, because it will influence your paycheck and title opportunities, and *your entire career.* So this isn't for the faint of heart, or for those who lack the courage of their convictions, but if you're ready to roll the bones, this is it.

Don't screw it up. Whatever this Big Thing is—managing an overseas office, creating a new trading desk, expanding a new banking division, overhauling the bank's entire accounting systems architecture—you have to pull it off. This means managing the project and process like a true professional and making sure you know the end game. If you do it, your name will be golden, and you'll be close to the peak. If you don't, you've probably had it. This is risk versus return in its most spectacular sense, so make sure you're ready to trade.

ADVERTISE YOUR SUCCESSES, DON'T ADVERTISE YOUR FAILURES

Like everyone else in the working world you're going to have good days and bad days. Some days everything will go like clockwork—everything gets done (and then some), you dazzle yourself, your colleagues, and your boss. Some days everything will be awful—when everything you touch explodes. That's okay, it's just part of life.

Remember that when things are going well, you've got to advertise your success. There is no room for modesty on Wall Street. This is a tough corporate environment, and you are going up against hundreds, even thousands, of colleagues in your race for MD, so you can't be shy about trumpeting your good work. If you've landed a new "big fish" client or deal, or discovered an operational problem and how to solve it, or uncovered a way of saving the firm lots of money every year, then some well-placed e-mails or memos to your boss (and maybe her boss, with a few useful "cc's" to others) are a good idea. Though you may not be comfortable telling the rest of the world what you've accomplished, too bad. Get over the discomfort, and start advertising your actions.

The opposite scenario doesn't hold true: you should never actively advertise your failures. No one likes it when things go wrong—not you, not your colleagues, not your boss, not her boss. If your failure looks temporary—if you can go back and "make it right" later in the day, or by next week—then keep quiet. No one needs to know that you screwed up. On your journey up the mountain you want to appear as infallible as possible, so the less that people know about your mistakes, the better. Of course there are times when your mistakes are a bit larger and you need to come clean (or somewhat clean). A confession to your boss is probably in order, but it should probably be understated (if you think you can get it all fixed up eventually). No need to get into the gory details, as they'll probably just become emblazoned in your boss's mind. The point is not to obfuscate or hide anything, but to spare your boss (and you) any undo stress or grief.

LEARN TO PLAY THE GAME—IT MATTERS

The unfortunate truth about working in the corporate world is that you have to play the game to get ahead. That's just the way it goes. It's part of taming the insecurity that lives in your boss (her boss, and her boss, and so on), and it's part of the politics of Wall Street. So you must always be prepared.

You play the game in different ways: by being overly enthusiastic and supportive when your boss comes up with a half-baked idea, by agreeing to do your boss a favor when he/she is in a bind, by giving your boss the credit for ideas you've developed or projects you've completed, by taking on unwanted jobs that no one wants to do, and so on. Find opportunities to be helpful from time to time (don't do it all the time—you just need a sprinkling every so often). Recognize that it's part of the price of getting ahead in a political environment. Imagine if you're always telling your boss he's wrong or his ideas are bad, or don't let him have credit for your work, or refuse to do the ugly job that no one else wants to do. How far will that get you?

Playing the game should never be your primary modus operandi because, taken to an extreme, it becomes transparent and degrading. You can spot the 100 percent game players from a long distance off—the yes-men and yes-women who regularly fetch the boss lunch and run his errands, who stay late to try and impress, who always support his initiatives (even the stupid ones) with unnecessary, and highly artificial, enthusiasm. These folks are wildly political, but basically can't do anything on their own (they are, however, dangerous and can make your life a bit difficult until their true colors are exposed—so be careful).

HAVING GODFATHERS AND GODMOTHERS HELPS

The godfather/mother network is alive and well on Wall Street—and it can help you on your long journey to the top. Godfathers/mothers are the well-respected, seasoned senior executives who take you (and others) under their wings—to nurture, protect, and promote. They may be family friends who helped you get your first job on The Street, or bosses/former bosses who keep an eye on you as you make your way through the firm and its hierarchy, or mentors you impressed during your analyst rotation program. They've probably developed a fondness for you and what you can contribute, so they are on the lookout for your best interests.

It's important for you to cultivate and reinforce these relationships. Take some time as you make your way through the firm to build relations with executives who might become godfathers/mothers, not because you want something specific, direct, and obvious from them, but because you know they can be important behind-the-scenes advocates, defenders, proponents, and supporters of your actions, activities, and career—especially as you get closer to making MD. When the going gets tough and the firm is heading through some bad times, godfathers/mothers can do their best to give you air cover, to protect you, to insulate you. When a new posting comes up in Tokyo or London that you think could be your Big Thing, godfathers/mothers can whisper a good word on your behalf to the right people. When your team's bonus pool is being decided, godfathers/mothers can tip the scales in your favor by telling the compensation panel about your group's enormous contributions. And, when it's time for promotion to the top rung, they can provide valuable lobbying and support.

The godfather/mother relationship is a strange beast on Wall Street because there is generally no quid pro quo—godfathers/mothers usually have what they want and are just trying to make sure hard-working talent keeps coming into the firm so that the place keeps getting better (and the share price keeps going up and, yes, their shareholdings become more valuable). Sure, they may occasionally ask a modest favor of you, but that's not their aim: they want to groom, sponsor and mentor those who have real potential. So develop your godfathers/mothers and treat them with respect.

PRAY THAT THE MD COMMITTEE LIKES YOUR WORK

At most Wall Street firms, MD titles are handed out only after extensive consultation between MDs and senior executives—people who know you, your work, accomplishments, reputation and character. This panel—the MD committee—usually consists of 10 to 15 senior executives from different areas: banking, trading, sales, accounting, risk. The committee typically meets once a year to review eligible candidates and discuss reasons why each should or shouldn't be admitted to the elite circle. Your future rests in the hands of these people.

By the time you are up for MD there is very little you can say or do that will influence the decision of the committee. If things are working properly, the sum total of your character, experience, accomplishments, and behavior over the years should speak for itself and should be the committee's main focus. Sure, some political forces can rear up—this is Wall Street, after all. If 9 of 10 MD openings have been decided and the head of investment banking wants to make sure one of her bankers, rather than a more deserving star trader, gets the last one, she may well play some political cards (e.g., call in some "favors" from other MD committee members, do some quiet "discrediting" of the other candidate, etc.). But that's why the committee comprises professionals from different disciplines, to minimize politics and make sure the process is as equitable as it can be. (Note that the MD committee also rubber stamps MD nominations of folks who join as MDs from competing firms. It's rare that a firm can hire an MD from down the block at a title other than MD. Who would want to go through that agonizing hell again?)

If your name is finally before the MD committee, there's nothing you can really do but pray. If you win the big prize, you're at the top. But if you don't make it, then there are two paths in front of you: resubmission or banishment. If you are lucky you might get resubmitted for consideration when you become eligible again. But you typically aren't eligible for two or three years. Those are the rules designed to keep executives from nominating too many people year after year and then just playing the law of averages. Resubmission happens when the committee feels you've got most of the desirable MD qualities the firm is looking for but need a bit more work in a particular area. It's a blow to the ego, to be sure, but buck up, find out where you went wrong, and make it your goal to fix it over the next 24 to 36 months. The second path, banishment, means you're probably damaged goods—decidedly not MD material. This becomes apparent when a majority of committee members vote against you and refuse to consider you as a candidate for resubmission. When this happens, you've hit the end of the line. The problem with your candidacy probably isn't one you can solve. The committee may feel that you lack the right attitude or personality, that you aren't good at working with others or treating clients properly, that you don't demonstrate proper support of the "corporate principles" (remember those?), and so on—in short, basic character flaws that, for most of us, are nearly impossible to change (after all, we are the way we are). If this happens you'll need to decide whether you want to remain a director for the rest of your career at the firm or try and find greener pastures down the block. That's a tough choice, and one that only you can make. Pray that you don't have to make it.

AND IN THE END, LUCK STILL MATTERS

Let's say you're the most talented and hardworking investment banker or trader in the universe. You work during a very long and hearty bull market and have the right political connections and a godmother looking out for you. You play the game just enough to make you appear cooperative and supportive.

You still need luck. That's frustrating if you want to be 100 percent in charge of your destiny, but it's true. Luck matters. You have to be in the right place at the right time, in the right job during the right market cycle. You have to have the right boss in the right part of the firm and have to complete the right Big Thing at exactly the right time if you want to reach the MD summit.

Luck matters when you are trying to scale the mountain. Do everything else you can to get yourself in the right spot—work hard, hit the road, get new clients, deliver the goods—and then hope that luck comes your way, because you still need it.

So, as you climb up the mountain there is a chance you will reach the peak and make MD if you are: *Patient* + *Talented* + *Exceptionally Hardworking* + *Politically Savvy* + *Lucky*. If the MD committee decides in your favor, congratulations! This is the job you've been trying to land for 10, 15, or 20 years. The prestige is almost tangible, the rewards and perks very considerable—and the continued responsibilities enormous. Remember, Wall Street is an "up or out" society—this isn't academia, and you don't have tenure. So you've got to come in tomorrow and keep being indispensable.

Lots of the rewards you get as an MD, indeed as any Wall Streeter, are tied specifically to the compensation process. And, as we mentioned at the start of the book, that's surely one of the main reasons you're on Wall Street, one of the reasons you've decided to be a cliff dweller. So let's see how compensation really works.

The Bottom Line: Bonuses

After you've spent a bit of time on Wall Street you'll realize why it's so fun and exciting. Where else can you get the thrill that comes from winning the big deal or the adrenaline rush that comes from pulling off a complicated client trade? Where else can you enjoy the great game of chess that you play to outwit the competition? Where else can you test your brains and courage by making daring investment research calls? Only on Wall Street.

On the other hand, where else can you find so many peculiar aggravations and stresses? So many 18-hour workdays? Weekends lost to conference calls, due diligence trips, and presentation preparations? Cross-country/global travel that wrecks your body, mind, and health? Politics, hatchet-throwing, back-stabbing, and infighting, all on a daily basis? Only on Wall Street.

Surely, you endure all this not just for the thrills of competing, the pride of a job "well done," or a pat on the back from your boss? Surely, it's not just for that burst of adrenaline? No. You do it for the dollars—lots and lots of them. That's the bottom line. It's why you're sacrificing yourself, and it's what motivates you and keeps you going when things get tough and ugly. You're doing all of this so you can earn a very good living and plan a future away from Wall Street's pressure cooker.

WHEN YEAR-END BONUS TIME COMES, BE VISIBLE

Wall Street compensation revolves around year-end bonuses and the entire process related to it. Sure, Wall Streeters get paid an annual salary just like other working folks, and most salaries are quite generous. By the time you make it to VP or director your salary will be more than what the average professional or corporate executive earns as total compensation. However, Wall Streeters treat monthly paychecks as so much pocket change, because their bonuses are multiples of their bases—100 percent, 500 percent, 1,000 percent, 5,000 percent of base, or more. That's a lot.

At most firms the bonanza comes in December or January, so it's important for you to be around, available, visible, and helpful, during this critical period. If you've thought about taking two or three weeks off in December when things slow down to go trekking in the Himalayas or yachting in the Mediterranean, forget it. Your place is in the office, near your boss, being supportive, in good spirits, and full of holiday cheer. If you're on an overseas assignment, this is a good time to get back to the Big Machine. You can create any excuse you want (e.g., "since I'm coming home for the holidays to see the folks, family, and friends, I think I'll just stop by the office for a few days to see how things are going"). Never mind that you aren't visiting folks, family, and friends at all. Just be close to the office/boss when the bonus numbers are starting to gel. (Note that this is also a good time to advertise. Remind your boss of some of the successes you've had during the year, and the great things you are already working on for next year.) Be visible because bonuses only happen once a year.

DIVVYING THE SPOILS BY SHOUTING MATCHES

So how does a firm figure out how much money is available for bonuses and who's going to get how much? The whole process is kind of like a mysterious tribal dance—one that begins slowly, builds steadily through regular crescendos, and then reaches a frenzied climax: the final allocation of bonus pools.

The first cut at the "high-level number" is based on how well the firm has done as a whole. If markets are good, and revenues are strong, the bonus pool for the entire firm will be equal to X (where X itself is based on certain percentages, market conventions, industry statistics, and—in the well-managed firm—some input from the board of directors). If markets are tough, or the firm has been trampled by the competition in its search for business, the pool might only be X/2 or X/4. Neither you nor your boss nor his boss (and maybe even his boss) has any control over X or the denominator.

Once the high-level number is set, the firm's top executive managers then engage in a series of shouting matches to get their share of X so that they can pay their people. They each need to try to get as much of the pool as possible so they can deliver good bonuses to their key players so they don't lose them to the bank down the block come February. The head of investment banking will make the case for trying to take 75 percent of X based on deals, revenues, bottom-line earnings, market share, talent retention, and so on. The head of trading will make the case for trying to take 75 percent of X based on the same rationale, the head of retail sales will do the same, and so forth. In fact, it is well known that every executive manager always wants 75 percent of X for his or her division. During these intense shouting matches, creative accounting often surfaces—accounting in which the sum of each division's earnings is far, far, far greater than the firm's total earnings. It's interesting how such numerate folks can come up with such silly figures.

After shouting themselves to exhaustion, the executive managers each walk away with some portion of X (which we will term x). Then come the divisional shouting matches. Within investment banking, the head of M&A will fight for 75 percent of x, the head of corporate finance will fight for 75 percent of x, the head of private equity will fight for the same, and so on. This scene will be repeated dozens, even hundreds of times, till your boss comes up with some portion of some portion of some portion of x that he can allocate to you and your colleagues. No wonder nothing happens on Wall Street in December except shouting.

THE BONUS RECIPE:
MIX MERIT, FAVORITISM, AND FEAR

After firm, division, and business unit pools have been decided (i.e., the little bits of x that still remain—which are still remarkably large), managers (including your boss) pull out the tried-and-true bonus recipe. This recipe combines equal parts merit, favoritism, and fear to produce some sort of tasty treat.

Merit is based on what you do during the year—all those deals, clients, trades, research reports, corporate projects, and team tasks that you've slaved over (and that you should have been advertising along the way). If you've done a good job (perhaps even completing one of the Big Things we talked about in chapter 9), you deserve to get paid. Since Wall Street preserves some element of meritocracy, one-third of your bonus should have some grounding in the reality of your actions and efforts. You can influence this dimension of the process by actually doing good work and letting your boss know. This part is entirely up to you.

Favoritism is a bit more difficult to influence because it demands a bit more politicking, a bit more game-playing. To be sure, your boss will favor you if you're a good performer, but she will *really* favor you if you're in the thick of things—doing some extra tasks (above and beyond the call of duty), providing support on important issues, being, in general, a yes- man or yes-woman, and making her look good. If you're selfish—refusing to play the game, devoted solely to your own work and accomplishments, and generally unwilling to provide your boss with the right kind of support—you're going to get dinged in this part of the process. So you can influence this part of the recipe if you are willing to play along. (This makes it a bit harder for overseas folks, so if you are an expat you have to make a much greater effort at communicating—e.g., daily calls, daily e-mails, and frequent trips—so that you can give your boss the same support as your Big Machine colleagues.)

The last part of the bonus recipe is based on fear. This is a difficult, far less tangible dimension, but it's just as important (as you can tell from the equal weighting it receives). Fear is the hold that you have—knowingly or unknowingly—over your boss, her boss, and her boss's boss, and it comes from *what you do, what you know,* and *whom you know,* and what you might do with all of that if you decide to leave. Think about it this way: if you are a star performer, producing constantly, working incessantly, and playing the game just right, your boss will come to believe that she can't afford to lose you to another department or, heaven forbid, another firm. Your departure would make her look bad *now* (i.e., unable to retain talent) and in the *future* (i.e., no one to step in and do the good work you've been doing). So, factored into your bonus payment will be some "retention" dollars tied to the fear of losing you (kind of like little handcuffs). This goes back to what we talked about in chapters 3 and 5 about being indispensable. If you're indispensable, you'll always do well on this part of the recipe. (Obviously, if you aren't indispensable and generate no fear, you get $0 on this piece.) There is also fear about what you know and whom you know. If you know your boss is weak in a particular area or has done something wrong (and she knows that you know), or if your boss knows that your godfather is the head of M&A or institutional trading, these elements will find their way into hard dollars come bonus time. You can influence all of this to a certain extent if you're confident in what you've done, what you know, or whom you know. For instance, over lunch with your boss you can drop subtle hints about other areas of the firm that seem interesting to you, or the fact that your boss's revenue estimates for December don't seem to match up with yours, or that you are having dinner next week with the head of M&A or institutional trading. As you drop the hint, watch your boss's cheeks. If there is redness or a flushed look, then you've probably just added a few dollars to your take-home pay.

EXCRUCIATING YEAR-END FICTION #2: PERFORMANCE REVIEWS

Since bonuses are one part merit, we need to talk about formal year-end merit evaluations (aka performance reviews). Merit evaluations, which are supposed to tell every employee at the firm how well or poorly they've done during the past 12 months, are another one of the Wall Street's great year-end fictions. Come December, your boss will give you a written and verbal review of all the good and bad things you've done over the past year, and if you've made it to the point where you have staff of your own, you'll have to do a few reviews of your own. A typical performance review sets forth goals that you're supposed to achieve during the year, how well you achieved them (if you did), and what you can do to improve on them next year. So around the beginning of December, expect to sit down with your boss to discuss the results (and then plan on doing the same with your subordinates).

But performance reviews are a fiction because they attempt to formalize, usually very poorly, what you, your subordinates, and your boss already know. On Wall Street you always know where you stand. It's reflected in daily conversations, in screaming matches, in praise, in criticism. You don't need a summarized, cookie-cutter personnel form to tell you what you're good at or where you're weak. You will know. Unfortunately, you've still got to go through the charade of a review based on human resource - supplied corporatespeak templates (the personnel folks need "something for the file"). So everyone ties to cram 250 business days' worth of activity, achievements, and failures into a two-page form, which gets discussed in 10 minutes (or less). And everyone uses the same descriptors and rejoinders, such as:

- "[Employee name here] performed diligently during the year. [He/ She] arranged [number] transactions and closed on [number] of them. The transactions contributed $[x] in fees to the firm's operating budget."
- "[Employee name here] is [well regarded/not well regarded] by his colleagues and subordinates. [He/she] [is/is not] an effective manager and [is/is not] always willing to provide guidance and support."
- "[Employee name here] [is/is not] hardworking and [has/does not have] a good eye for detail."
- "In order for [employee name here] to continue to progress at the firm, [he/she] should be given additional management responsibilities and go for one week of [leadership/ethics/computer] training."

So what does the process really tell you, your manager, or anyone else? Nothing at all. In fact, since everyone recognizes the fact that the whole thing is useless, don't be surprised if your boss asks you to do your own review. It's called a "self-review," "self-assessment," or "self-critique," and it means your boss, recognizing the fiction, would rather do something else with his time. When you're done evaluating yourself your boss will give it a quick glance, agree with it, and then pop off to do some last-minute shopping for the holidays (no one does any year-end deals because the clients are all on vacation).

THE GUILT OF A BIG BONUS FADES QUICKLY

Wall Street pay scales are unreal, without any grounding in reality. The sums that are paid to all eligible Wall Streeters, from analysts to MDs, are stratospheric when times are good, and still pretty handsome when they're not so good. This gives rise to inner conflict and turmoil: elation when you open the year-end paycheck and find that you now have a lot more disposable income than you ever thought possible, and guilt over the fact that what you've just been paid, in a single paycheck, is more than your parents earned in 10, 15, or 25 years of really hard work.

The elation lasts a very short time, particularly when you've been on The Street for a while. The guilt lingers a little longer, but you still get over it pretty quickly. Right or wrong, you start to rationalize, and then justify, your pay, maybe because it helps soothe the conscience. You'll think of all the long hours you put in during the year, all the lost weekends, all the sleepless nights on airplanes, all the violent shouting matches on the trading floor, all the "white knuckle moments" while you were waiting for a deal to come through, all the Mylanta you drank to calm your upset stomach, all the coffee you drank to stay awake. You let all of these thoughts fly around your brain for a while, and you'll actually come to a point where any notion of guilt is gone, and you actually think you deserve what you've been given. The mind works in mysterious ways!

Then you'll go through it all over again during the next bonus season—the same elation, the same feeling of guilt, the same let-me-justify-my-pay thought cycle. Even in bad years, when the paycheck isn't quite as large, it's still large enough to make you feel kind of bad, but only for a little while.

SPOILED AND JADED

The most exciting compensation moment you're likely to have on Wall Street—either as a new graduate or as a business professional moving onto The Street—happens when you get your very first bonus check. Assuming Wall Street is not in some horribly depressing cyclical downturn, that first paycheck will give you the biggest thrill you'll ever have, so cherish it.

Why the most exciting? Because it'll be a new experience for you and unlike anything you're accustomed to. Your year-end bonus up to then is likely to have ranged from $0 (if you've been in school) to maybe 5 percent or 10 percent of your annual salary (if you've been slaving away at some other noble profession). So when you open that first Wall Street bonus check (discreetly, when no one's looking), and you see that it's 50 percent, 100 percent, or 200 percent of your annual salary, you'll feel numb, your heart will beat faster, your face will get flushed. If you work on the trading floor or don't have your own office yet, you'll go off into the hallway or an empty conference room, anywhere you can be alone for a few minutes to savor the mix of pride, guilt, and excitement. You'll start daydreaming about what you'll do with the money and wait anxiously for the day to be over so you can go and tell your spouse, significant other, parents, kids, whomever.

And it'll never feel the same again.

Sure, you'll make lots more money over the years. If you're good, by the time you've spent 5, 10, or 15 years on The Street, you'll be getting some really big paychecks. They'll be so big, in fact, that you'll wonder how you ever managed to get by on the early ones. That first one will seem kind of pitiful and laughable. By then, you'll be spoiled and jaded. By then the Wall Street compensation reality won't be alien. It'll be your reality, the only one you've been living for a while. It'll be the only pay scale that makes sense to you. As a jaded Wall Street vet, you'll have been spoiled by big checks and come to expect big numbers. Year after year. You'll never be surprised on the upside, only on the downside—when you don't get what you want or think you should get (and then you'll be temporarily depressed, or will actually go and complain). So enjoy that first one. It will always be your most pleasant compensation memory.

GOOD STAFFERS CAN
OUTEARN MEDIOCRE PRODUCERS

It's a Wall Street truism that, given equal talent and experience, those who produce get paid more than those who staff or control. That's because, as we discussed in chapter 4, producers generate revenues for the firm, while staffers simply absorb some of those revenues (they are corporate overhead or expense items, albeit necessary ones, if the firm is managing itself properly). The producer adds direct value by bringing hard dollars in the door through deals, trades, and client relationships, while the staffer adds indirect value by making sure that dollars coming in the door aren't then mislaid or squandered. So both are important, but the hard link between dollars brought in means producers get paid more.

Producers also have far less job security than their staff colleagues. They are living even closer to the edge of the cliff. Bad markets, lack of transaction flow, some bad trades, or a few lost deals can spell the end of a producer's career. That's not necessarily true of staffers, who are generally much more insulated, living a bit farther away from the edge of the precipice. Someone still has to keep the books, do the audits, and look after the technology, regardless of how business is faring. So it follows from the risk/return equation we talked about earlier that the relative lack of job security commands a higher risk premium—payable in the form of a larger bonus. Remember, there can be no "free lunch." If you want more return, you have to take more risk.

But there actually is a bit of a free lunch out there. Though it's true that producers earn more than staffers, an *excellent* staffer can earn more than a mediocre producer, and sometimes almost as much as a good producer. So if you strive to be an excellent staffer (and this truly means excellent, on the ball, full of good ideas and energy, and brilliant execution), want almost total job security, and are content earning 90 percent of what a decent producer will earn (without any of the year-to-year paycheck volatility that the producer faces) you will do very well for yourself without the stress of potential job loss. So a partial free lunch is available to qualified people who are interested.

SQUEAKY WHEELS USUALLY GET OILED

There are two compensation camps on Wall Street: one manned with soldiers who accept what they're given in their bonus envelopes, and another with soldiers who *never* accept what they're given. The latter features troopers who will burst into their boss's offices and demand more pay. They'll do this if they think they deserve more based on the work they've done or if they've heard that a colleague has earned more (and simply can't handle the thought of living in the knowledge that someone has gotten more regardless of work or merit). And some will do this even if they are totally satisfied with their pay—just as a sort of game. Nothing ventured, nothing gained, so why not? Some people apparently have no shame.

It often works. Unless times are especially lean, bosses usually comply, oiling the squeaky wheels so they don't have to hear them squeak anymore. Though they try to do the oiling quietly and discreetly, the squeaky wheels can generally be heard boasting down by the water cooler, so it tends not to be a secret for too long. Of course there are times when an honest mistake has been made, and the squeaking and oiling are justified, but more often it's just about people trying to get whatever they can from the firm.

EVEN IN BAD TIMES, GOOD PEOPLE GET PAID WELL

You can't expect to hit the jackpot year after year when you're on The Street unless you're really special. Assuming, just for a moment, that you're not really special, you've got to expect a few down years. Times when the markets are rough and clients are on sidelines, or when business is slow and the whole industry is chasing the same handful of paltry deals, or when you're just not doing a great job (hey, it happens). You shouldn't get discouraged, because you'll still get paid buckets more than anyone you know who's not working on The Street. Unless you're doing an awful job, you can always expect something. There's just no such thing as "sorry, kid, no bonus this year" on Wall Street (if you're doing a terrible job, you'll just get fired). Remember, too, that you're in it for the long haul. If you figure that, on average, you'll get "paid down" one out of every five years because of bad markets, and you plan on having a 20-year banking career, then you'll still have 16 good ones. That's a lot, especially when you consider that each one of those 16 year-end checks has five or six (maybe even seven) zeros on it.

But, if you really are special, you don't even have to worry about the other four "lean years." No Wall Street firm worth its salt will ever risk losing one of its top people through lack of compensation. Even when things are very bleak, the firm will manage to dig into some special treasure chest it's got hidden away up in the corporate attic so that it can compensate its stars well. People in executive management typically view this as "investing in the future." Though they may have to tighten the belt a bit, cut a few costs elsewhere, curtail travel and entertainment, they cannot, and will not, risk losing key players over a few bonus dollars (well, okay, more than a few). That would be shortsighted. If the firm can't pay its head industrial investment banker (a renowned rainmaker) enough one year, someone else down the block will, and she'll walk. If it can't properly pay the 15-person junk-bond team that is the envy of all of Wall Street, there is always some other firm that will go to the well and hire them away. Whenever good people are lost, firms have to replace or rebuild, losing precious time, money, and resources.

So if you happen to be in that elite group of special folks who are recognized as vital to revenues and franchise growth, expect to be paid well, whatever the market cycle. If you aren't part of that group, you may want to figure out what you need to do to join it.

THE "MANAGING EXPECTATIONS" SPEECH

Every so often (e.g., one out of every five years) things on The Street are pretty bleak, and money just doesn't flow through the door. That means something's got to give. If the Big Machine has already done its hatchet swinging and lopped off a few (dozen, hundred, or thousand) heads, eliminated lots of unnecessary costs accumulated during the fast times/fat times period, kicked out all of the part-timers and external consultants (aka leeches), then there's only one place it can turn: the bonus pool.

The bonus pool is the last thing that anyone wants to touch. It's the sacred cow that has to be protected at all costs because, as we've said, if you can't pay your folks, there's probably someone else who can (even when things are bleak all over The Street).

You'll probably have some inkling that things aren't going very well when you start getting interoffice memos telling you about new cost-cutting efforts. No more free cappuccinos on the trading floor, no more "waiting time" paid for limos, no travel without your boss's okay (and everyone, even the investment bankers, has to fly economy), no more hiring, and no holiday party. If the year is shaping up to be pretty lousy, these memos usually start circulating around midyear and continue steadily through December.

You'll become a bit more aware of the severity of the cycle when the pink slips start floating around and some of your buddies over in foreign exchange or leveraged transactions suddenly disappear. Here today, gone tomorrow; such is the life of the cliff dweller.

You'll know that things are really bad—and that the sacred cow isn't sacred anymore—when your boss calls you into her office to give you the "managing expectations" speech. This is a speech that everyone in the firm, except the elite folks we talked about above, gets when things are bad. It's the one in which your boss tells you that the firm is having a rough time and that management is doing everything it can to keep costs down and remain competitive. Though you are a valuable player, the speech goes, this year you really shouldn't expect to get paid as much. But just stick with us, your boss says, and next year will be better. All this is just a mental preparation so that you won't get really angry when you open your bonus check and won't try and do something drastic, like leave. You should plan on getting this speech around October or November, once third-quarter numbers have gelled and executive management has figured out how ugly things are. If you get the speech in early August, after second-quarter numbers come in, then things are going to be extremely ugly. Better just write the year off. Carry on, though, and remember that it's only one out of five.

IF YOU HAVE FAITH IN THE FIRM, TAKE THE OPTIONS

A portion of every Wall Streeter's bonus check is made up of stock options, which grant the right to buy a share of the firm at a particular price sometime in the future. Lots of younger folks (e.g., analysts/associates) groan when they find out that 20 percent to 60 percent of their bonuses come in the form of stock options instead of the sweet green, but they've got it all wrong. Stock options are a great way to get rich. You just have to be patient.

If you could have $1,000 today or $10,000, with 70 percent certainty, three years from now, which would you take? Unless you can invest in something turbo-charged that you think will hit the jackpot (which is likely to include lots of risk), you'd be a fool not to take the second alternative. So who cares if you don't have the $1,000 in hand now to buy something? If you wait for three years, you're 70 percent sure to have enough to buy 10 times more. Sure, you'd like to have everything right now and, yes, there is a 30 percent chance that you won't get $10,000 in three years—maybe you'll only get $2,000 or $5,000 (or, if things are really, really bad, maybe $0)—so why not take a chance and wait?

Options are actually one of the best things about Wall Street compensation packages (along with the sheer size of the packages, of course). They are a great and easy way to multiply your wealth—you just have to be very patient in exercising them. If you have faith in the firm, if you think the company is sound, well managed, has a good business strategy and franchise, and will be around for the long haul, take whatever you can in options. Naturally, there are market cycles that will pummel the stock and make that pile of options you're sitting on worthless—but that's only temporary. Over the medium term the market bounces back and, when it does, well-managed Wall Street firms (and their stock prices) come bouncing right back as well.

Most Wall Street firms give out options that last up to 10 years, so the chances that you'll see a strong bull market and a strong company stock price over that period are excellent—your pile will be okay. Just forget you own them, and keep working hard. After a few years you can slowly start exercising them—calmly and quietly. Never try to shoot for some "market high" on the stock price when you're starting to cash out. Don't be greedy, just have a logical plan for liquidating pieces of your pile. That will give you the cash reserve you need to start planning for your retirement, as we'll see in the next chapter.

A word of caution: options are really for those committed to staying at a particular firm for the long-haul—10 or 15 years or more. Most firms use options as a form of "retention"—financial handcuffs to get you to stick around because you can usually only vest and exercise 20 percent or 25 percent of your options per year. There are exceptions to this rule. If you've reached a certain age and put in enough time, you might automatically vest all of your options. Or, if you're a real superstar and want to go to the competing firm down the block, you can usually get your pile bought out and replaced by the competitor (you've got to be really good to get this kind of treatment, though). Otherwise, you've got to be patient and put in your time. Sound familiar?

BE GRATEFUL

When all is said and done, whatever you get paid on bonus day, be grateful. Sure, you've worked hard, you've sacrificed your personal life and maybe a bit of your health, you've put other interests and obligations on the back burner, all in the name of your job and your career. Still, you are very well paid. Even in down years, you are probably making much more than 90 percent, 95 percent, or 99 percent of the people living in your hometown, city, or state. For that you should be grateful.

So even though you expect to get a big paycheck year after year, never take it for granted. Just think how lucky you really are. Think how lucky you are that you've got a job that pays you so much that you can actually think about retiring early.

CHAPTER ELEVEN

Exit, Stage Left:
Retiring as Soon as Possible

The money you earn on Wall Street allows you to buy all the goodies you need, send your kids to decent schools, live in a good house, and drive a fancy car. But, in the middle of all that spending, you should always be thinking about the end game, retirement—more specifically, *early* retirement.

For lots of people, the days of working till 62, 65, or 70 are gone. Not for everyone—it takes a real asset base and some serious planning to be able to retire early and do it properly. But there are more than a few people, still quite young, who have done their Wall Street gig, left with pots of money, and are now doing things that they think are even more fun and interesting. There are many others who don't have quite as much, but are willing to trade in a high-cost/high-maintenance lifestyle for a simpler but very comfortable one—especially if that means getting out of the workforce 5, 10, or 15 years earlier than originally planned. This phenomenon is not limited to Wall Street, of course, but it's a lot easier for Wall Streeters because of the size of their annual cash bonuses and the ever-growing pile of options they accumulate.

Of course, not everybody wants to retire early. Some people genuinely enjoy going to work every day: keeping a routine, contributing, learning, interacting, socializing. Work is life, life is work. This applies to all industries, including Wall Street, and there's nothing wrong with that. More power to you if you can't imagine not going to work. But assuming you don't fall in this camp, that you aren't one of the hard-core Wall Street deal junkies that needs a daily, weekly, or monthly M&A fix, or a trader that doesn't know when to say "when," or an accountant or operations specialist that lives and breathes the daily transactions, you've got to plan for your exit from the stage. This means knowing how much you'll need in order to quit and what you're going to do once you quit. Depending on your job, experience, and the specific market cycle you happen to be in, you've got to plan on putting in 15 to 25 years of very hard Wall Street labor before you can retire. And there are certain things that you need to keep in mind while preparing for this.

CALCULATE WHAT YOU NEED, GET IT, AND GET OUT

As you head down the path toward retirement—and as it becomes more reality than fantasy—you need to do some hard math. Boot up that Excel spreadsheet program from your analyst days and put together a detailed budget of what you need in order to live comfortably for the rest of your years—how much you'll have coming in from your pile of assets, and how much you'll have going out—on housing, food, utilities, transportation, entertainment, education, taxes. Then run a bunch of "what if" scenarios—just as if you were analyzing cash flow projections on a corporate takeover deal—so that you can see just how sensitive you are to changes in your budgeted spending rate, interest rates, inflation, college tuition, tax rates, medical insurance premiums, and so on. Then figure out how much cash buffer you need to set aside for emergencies (e.g., one, two, five years of extra dollars). Then add a 25 percent to 50 percent cushion as your margin of error, depending on how liberal or conservative you are. Once you are truly convinced you know how much you will need to sustain a given retirement lifestyle, *make that your goal.*

Obviously, you've got to work really hard to achieve your goal: by doing a great job on The Street, of course, but also by spending prudently and saving aggressively. This doesn't mean you have to live like a pauper or not do/get the things you want. There's not much point in being so austere that you can't enjoy your life. It just means you shouldn't be foolish. If this all sounds a bit like your parents, good. It's supposed to, because they were right.

Once you're committed to your goal, and start amassing your fortune, *stick to it.* This is actually much harder than it seems, because many get caught up in the game, the thrill, the prestige, and the lifestyle that The Street offers. You might say you'll retire in five or ten years and, when that time has come, put it off for another two or three or five years—because you think you're having too much fun (maybe/maybe not) or you like the dollars/cachet/prestige (probably). There's nothing wrong with sticking around longer if that's always been your goal. If you want to work on Wall Street until you're 70, good for you, but if that's not really your goal, and you are just shifting your retirement so that you can hang on and squeeze out a little bit more jack, be careful. Before you know it you'll have lost a few more years of your life, all in pursuit of some extra dollars that probably won't make any real difference to you anyway.

Goals are useless unless you set them and stick to them. Don't get caught up in the Wall Street game and get carried away if that's not your goal. Just walk away when it's time to walk away.

MAKE HAY WHILE THE SUN IS SHINING

You're only going to make serious dollars while you are working. Once you quit you'll have to rely on income being generated by your assets and/or some part-time/consulting/freelance work to pay the bills and to buy all the fun stuff. That means you've got to maximize your earnings while you are part of the Wall Street workforce.

In practical terms this means sacrificing yourself for the job and the firm. You've got to be 100 percent dedicated to the idea of doing a great job so that your achievements get noticed and recognized, and so that you get promoted from analyst to VP to MD, earning more and saving more. There is no sense in being on Wall Street if you aren't going to do everything you can to maximize your earnings. If you're half-hearted about the idea and give it only half the effort, then your work will be mediocre, your pay will be mediocre, and you will be slaving away until you're 65. Remember what we said in chapter 2: know exactly why you want to be on Wall Street and then give it all you've got. If your goal is to retire early, then give it all you've got, every single day. If this sounds like something a pro football coach tells his team before the big game, or what a motivational speaker might say at the corporate rah-rah event, good. It's supposed to, because they are right.

TAKE SOME CHIPS
OFF THE TABLE BEFORE YOU RETIRE

We've talked about how good options can be for your wealth-building plan, and how important it is to be patient in turning them into cash. If the markets are strong and the firm is doing well, then the longer you wait, the more you'll earn. But if you're going to quit early, you need to be wise about your option exercises and start taking some chips off the table before you quit. Sure, you've got to figure out all the tax angles first, but then you've got to come up with a regular schedule for turning a piece of your options pile into cash so that you can reinvest in some other things, things that aren't related to Wall Street or the firm. You need to diversify.

Imagine that you have 95 percent of your wealth tied up in options on the firm's stock, accumulated through tremendously hard work over a 15-year period. Imagine, also, that you wait for your retirement day to start cashing out most of what you've got. Imagine, finally, that another October 1987 crash comes around while you're having cocktails at your retirement party, but before you actually exercise your options. As the firm's stock hits a new multiyear low, you're in deep trouble. Most of your options are now probably worthless (and might remain so for a few years, till the market claws its way back up), and most of your wealth has vanished. That's when you find yourself begging your boss to let you come back and work for a few more years.

So the lesson is to be patient when exercising your options, but have a plan for regularly lightening the load—turning your paper wealth into real wealth—and reinvesting in other things.

DON'T INVEST LIKE A RECKLESS TRADER

If you've spent the past 10 or 20 years as a high-stakes investment banking deal maker, or an aggressive, in-your-face "give me more risk" bond trader, or a slick, big-ticket-only institutional salesperson, you undoubtedly like the thrill of the deal. You probably enjoy risk and taking chances (and you're probably one of those folks that goes in for base-jump parachuting, ultra-ultra-marathons, sheer-face glacier-climbing, and suspension bridge bungee jumping). But remember, you've spent the past few decades risking the firm's resources, not your own. Money lost on bad trades or by not winning deal fees or sales commissions comes out of the firm's checkbook, not yours. Sure, there's always an element of personal down-side—if you have a few bad years as a trader or deal maker, you'll get paid less and have less to show for your attempts. But Wall Street is pretty forgiving. If you punt and get it wrong, you'll still get paid decently and can have another try next year.

This means you need to develop a different attitude toward risk when you're dealing with your own assets. You can't buy investments that will blow up once you've retired—no leveraged inverse floaters or CMO z-tranches or emerging market stocks bought on margin. Keep it simple and generally conservative (okay, so you can have a little high-risk fund for playing games with financial toxic waste, but this has to be really small—and when your little high-risk fund is on a hot streak, you shouldn't succumb to temptation to divert resources from your conservative fund to play more games). You have to bury your previous risk tendencies in favor of something that will keep the income stream smooth and steady. It's boring, to be sure, but you shouldn't be tampering with your retirement assets and income. If you want the thrill of the risk, go parachuting.

THE GUILT OF NOT WORKING PASSES

If you've planned this thing out right and put in your years of hard work, you'll wake up one morning and realize that you don't have to scramble to catch a subway, cab, bus, or train. You don't have to stuff a bagel in your mouth as you run from the elevator to the trading floor. You don't have to show up for any more crack-of-dawn-so-we-can-catch-Tokyo conference calls, and you don't have to spend long hours ensconced with lawyers, accountants, or regulators in a windowless room. You don't have to haul out to the airport to catch yet another flight to see yet another client. You don't have to write any more trade tickets or figure out how your positions are faring. You don't even need to know if stocks, bonds, currencies (or anything else) are going up or down!

You don't have to do anything. Wow.

The freedom, the liberty. No responsibilities—your time is your own (well, generally speaking: you'll be doing lots of other things that you didn't plan on doing, like home projects, errands, shopping, chauffeuring, but that's another book).

Prepare yourself, because it's an odd, bittersweet feeling—a mix of emotions. The unbelievable sense of freedom, combined with the confusion that comes with being disconnected and out of the mainstream (you will have relinquished your cell phone and Blackberry already). And there is guilt. If you're still young and still have energy and drive, you'll wonder why you're not working, just like everyone else.

Make no mistake, this new life takes getting used to. You will have to come to grips with these conflicting feelings, which is why it is important to plan what you'll do with your free time before you actually have free time. However, the feelings of guilt slowly fade, particularly as you find fun and valuable things to do. Don't beat yourself up too much. More important, *don't give in to the dark side*. You can't go back to Wall Street. You've worked really hard to get to this point, so you shouldn't feel like you're bad, idle, a pariah. The guilt will eventually pass. For some it takes weeks, others months and still others years, and then you'll hit your post–Wall Street stride, and everything will seem all right. Have patience.

PLAN WHAT TO DO BEFORE YOU RETIRE

To minimize the shock of not working and to assuage any feelings of guilt, uselessness, and disconnection, you need to have a one-year plan before you actually leave The Street. This will give you meaning, direction, and a daily schedule, which are important once you realize that you don't *have* to be anywhere and you don't *have* to do anything. Though the freedom is fun and, by definition, liberating, you still need structure.

Your plan should include fun things that you've always wanted to do but haven't been able to because you've been hard at work on Wall Street. Your sacrifice has been total, so it's time to rediscover the fact that there are fun things out there to do. This may involve learning a new skill, like yachting or piano or Japanese. It may mean going somewhere interesting or exotic for an extended period, or it may mean something as simple as reading and watching movies. Enjoy the fun things by making them part of your plan.

But your plan should also include serious things that will keep your mind sharp and make you feel that you're still a contributing member of society. Maybe this means you should teach classes at the local community college or university, do volunteer work for some nonprofit organization, or do part-time consulting work related to your field of expertise. Or maybe you can write some articles or books, learn how to program in C++ or Java, or refresh your calculus skills. Anything that you can do regularly that will give you an intellectual challenge. If you don't feature something serious in your one-year plan, you'll get restless and antsy, and wonder why you've actually abandoned Wall Street, and that's scary. The serious side of your one-year plan may also give you a fresh outlook on a possible second career. Though you won't want to work from 7 A.M. to 8 P.M. every day in the intense Wall Street scene, you may want to work from 10 A.M. to 3 P.M. or just a few days a week or month in a low-pressure, low-stress area that interests you. Not because you need to, but because you want to.

Once you've completed your first year of retirement, things will start to look, sound and feel different. You'll develop a routine that makes sense, and you'll enjoy yourself, but you'll also learn and grow. Sure, you'll miss Wall Street a bit, but then you'll come to realize that there is more to life than just deals, prices, accounts, and clients. You'll watch CNBC a little less often, you'll read the *Wall Street Journal* less frequently, and as time goes by you won't really miss it all that much. By the time you enter your second, third, and fourth years of retirement, your daily plan will be second nature, and you'll have an entirely different rhythm to your day and life.

MAINTAIN GOOD RELATIONS WITH EX-COLLEAGUES

Keep in touch with your former colleagues. They will always be an important link to your past, and, though you shouldn't necessarily want to live in the past, you no doubt shared good and bad times with them and developed a strong bond, and that is worth something.

You might also want to remain plugged into what's going on because hearing about the politics, infighting, backstabbing, bad elephant hunting seasons, and the invariable deal-gone-sour-at-the-last-moment will make you realize that you don't really miss all the headaches and that you made the right decision to walk away (with a bit of your health and youth left!). Remember, also, that ex-colleagues may become future business clients or partners if you decide to go out on your own and do some consulting work, set up an investment fund, or tap into the Wall Street scene in some other way. So don't lose touch with them.

ENJOY LIFE

In the end, you should enjoy yourself. As we said at the start of this little book, that's what it's all about. Life is short, so try to make the most of it. *Carpe diem.*

If you land on Wall Street, learn about the financial business, work through good times and tough times, dodge the political bullets, land some nice deals, contribute and add value, do well, earn dollars, and manage your affairs properly, you'll be able to do what many still only dream about: quit working at an age where you're still young enough to live the rest of your life the way you want to. And you'll have learned and experienced an awful lot along the way.

It doesn't come easy. You've got to put in lots and lots of effort, bide your time, pick your battles, and work your way up. And as we've said several times, you need Lady Luck to shine on you a few times.

But if all of these things happen, then working The Street will have been a worthwhile journey.

Good luck.